Charlton Kings Church

THE OLD PARISH CHURCHES
OF GLOUCESTERSHIRE
Mike Salter

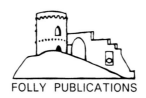

FOLLY PUBLICATIONS

ACKNOWLEDGEMENTS

The photographs and measured drawings in this book are mostly the product of the author's fieldwork between 1971 and 2008. Old postcards and brass rubbings are reproduced from originals in the author's collections. Thanks are due to Paul Adkins, Simon Rose, and Helen Thomas for help with transport on field-trips in Gloucestershire, to Allan and Paul at Aspect Design for help in putting the artwork of the book together, and to my mother Marjorie Salter for checking through the text.

ABOUT THIS BOOK

As with the other books in this series (see full list on the inside of the back cover) this book concentrates on the period before the Industrial Revolution of the late 18th century. Most furnishings and monuments after 1800 are not mentioned, but additions and alterations to the fabric usually are, although in less detail. Churches founded after 1800 to serve new suburban areas do not appear in the gazetteer or on the map.

The Forest of Dean churches have already been fully described and illustrated in a separate volume first published in 1990 and this material is not repeated here. The churches of South Gloucestershire will be described in a later volume of this series, along with those of Bristol. Leaving out these two areas has resulted in a book of more manageable size and a map that more easily fits onto one page without being small.

The book is inevitably very much a catalogue of dates and names, etc. It is intended as a field guide and for reference rather than to be read straight from cover to cover. Occasionally there is a comment about the setting of a church but on the whole not much is said about their locations or atmosphere. Also, notable features of a few of the buildings may lie outside the scope of this book. Visit them and judge for yourself. The book is intended to be used in conjunction with the O.S. 1:50,000 scale Landranger maps and a two letter and six figure grid reference appears after each place-name and dedication. The numbers of the maps required are: 149, 150, 151, 162, 163, 173.

Plans redrawn from originals in the author's notebooks are reproduced to a common scale of 1:400, with the exception of that of Tewkesbury Abbey, which has had to be made smaller to fit onto a single page. The buildings were measured in metres and only metric scales are given. Three metres almost equals ten feet for those still wanting imperial measures. A hatching system common to all the plans is used to denote the different periods of work. Note that some things are difficult on convey on small scale plans (eg stones of one period being reset or reused in a later period). In some cases walling is shown on a plan as being of a specific century when it is in fact difficult to date with accuracy. There are for instance several towers that may be either late 14th or early 15th century.

ABOUT THE AUTHOR

Mike Salter is 54 and has been a professional author and publisher since 1988. He is particularly interested in the planning and layout of medieval buildings and has a huge collection of plans of castles and churches he has measured during tours (mostly by bicycle and motorcycle) throughout all parts of the British Isles since 1968. Wolverhampton born and bred, Mike now lives in an old cottage beside the Malvern Hills. His other interests include walking, maps, railways, board games, morris dancing and playing percussion instruments and calling folk dances with an occasional folk group.

First published March 2008. Copyright 2008 Mike Salter.
Folly Publications, Folly Cottage, 151 West Malvern Rd, Malvern, Worcs WR14 4AY
Printed by Aspect Design, 89 Newtown Rd, Malvern, Worcestershire WR14 2PD

Dymock Church

CONTENTS

INTRODUCTION

Until Gloucester Abbey was made a cathedral and the seat of a new bishopric in 1540 the county of Gloucester lay within the diocese of Worcester founded in 679. The two counties of Gloucestershire and Worcestershire were later formed from what had been the kingdom of the Hwicce. When Christianity was introduced to this area is uncertain. No large-scale conversion is recorded in Saxon times and it may perhaps have survived from late Roman times. During the Saxon period the aristocracy founded minster churches which served large areas approximating to the hundreds. In the area covered by this book minster churches existed at Berkeley, Bibury, Bishop's Cleeve, Blockley, Daylesford, Deerhurst, Gloucester, Tetbury, Withington, and perhaps Bisley and Twyning. The minsters were monastic but also served as parish churches.

Gloucestershire is actually quite rich in remains of Saxon churches. Much survives at Deerhurst, first recorded in 804 and extended in several campaigns over the next hundred years or so to produce a wide nave with an east apse to contain the main altar and a series of porticus or side-chapels with lesser altars, whilst what began as a west porch was later continued up as a tower. Footings have been revealed of an even larger fully aisled basilica at Cirencester which was later replaced by the Norman abbey church. At Gloucester another Norman abbey church replaced a Saxon minster of which little is known. Minor fragments of a second minster known to have had a rare west apse remain at the nearby priory of St Oswald. There are substantial remains of a large late 10th or early 11th century nave and chancel church at Bisley. Original features are the chancel arch, pilaster buttresses and one circular window in the nave.

Smaller churches and chapels-of-ease were soon provided to supplement the minsters. The nave at Somerford Keynes has a doorway with a stilted arch which may be 8th century. The stones used 'to make this opening go through the whole wall thickness. The naves at Ampney Crucis, Daglingworth, Duntisbourne Abbots, Duntisbourne Rouse, and Miserden are all of Saxon origin, characteristic features being alternate long and short stones at the corners, round-arched doorways, and herringbone masonry with courses of slabs laid diagonally. More complete nave and chancel churches remain at Coln Rogers and Odda's Chapel at Deerhurst, both with small round-arched windows preserved, those at Deerhurst being set midway in the wall-thickness with wide internal external splays. This chapel is precisely dated to the 1050s and it is likely that the others are also early to mid 11th century, i.e. Late Saxon, but dating is uncertain and herringbone masonry was used up until c1140. Another building of this period survives in use as a barn close to the Norman priory church at Leonard Stanley. In addition to structural remains there are fragments of Saxon sculpture in the form of panels, grave-slabs or cross-shafts at about a dozen places, notably the statue of the Risen Christ at Beverston, and the three panels at Daglingworth, and at Lypiatt in the parish of Bisley is an 8th century cross not accompanied by a church or chapel.

Saxon window at Coln Rogers

Saxon window, Ampney St Mary   *Norman window at Ozleworth*   *Double lancets at Shipton Oliffe*

Gloucestershire is a rich county for remains of churches of the Norman period between 1066 and 1200. Of over 260 churches described in this book about 160 have a nave or a chancel or both which is of Saxon or Norman origin, even if much rebuilt or remodelled in later periods, and of the remaining hundred or so churches another 30 have a single doorway, chancel arch, arcade, font, or carved fragmets remaining from the Norman period. Up in the Cotswold hills nearly every church has something remaining from the 11th and 12th centuries.

Capitals at Bibury

Firstly there are two abbey churches at Gloucester and Tewkesbury which although remodelled in the 14th century still retain their Norman layout and form of a long nave with side aisles, a central tower with a transept on either side with eastern chapels. and an east end with an aisled ambulatory off which led three apsidal chapels. The abbey church at Gloucester became a cathedral in 1540 and does not further concern us here as the town had several other parish churches, but part of the abbey church at Tewkesbury was used by the townsfolk, who took over the whole building when the monastery was dissolved. Leonard Stanley has a nearly complete smaller Norman monastic church where again parishioners used the nave and later took over the whole building. It also is cruciform with a central tower, but there are no aisles and no projecting chapels remain, although two once existed east of the transepts. Cirencester had a cruciform Norman parish church in addition to the nearby abbey church, and a tiny cruciform church remains at Stowell, whilst Bishop's Cleve has remains of a cruciform church with an aisled nave. The churches of St Mary de Lode and St Mary de Crypt at Gloucester and St Mary at Cheltenham seem to have assumed their present cruciform layout by 1200 although not much Norman work survives in them. Other churches took the more usual two-celled form of a nave in which the concregation stood (seating only came into fashion later), and a small chancel just big enough to contain an altar and an attendant priest. The churches did vary quite a lot in size, those in the Vale of Severn such as Dymock and Hartpury sometimes having quite large naves, whilst some of those in the Cotswolds only ever served small congregations and were quite small.

Coln St Dennis Church

Norman window and wall-paintings at Kempley

Most Norman parish churches were dimly lighted by a few small round-headed windows set in deep embrasures. A few had somewhat larger windows and occasionally these were flanked externally by an order of shafts. Windows in naves are usually set quite high up, sometimes above an external or internal stringcourse. Just below the eaves of the roof some churches had a row of decoratively carved corbels known as a corbel table, as at Elkstone. Usually there would be doorways on the south and north sides of the nave. West doorways appear occasionally but are more normal in larger parish churches, abbeys, and cathedrals. The provision of a third doorway giving the priest his own direct access into the chancel without having to go through the nave only seems to have come into fashion around 1200. Norman doorways are very common amongst the churches in the Cotswolds. Some are fairly simple round arched openings, sometimes with the arch decorated with a roll-moulding which might occasionally have beakheads biting it, and often there are shafts on either side. Quite commonly a lintel is provided in addition to a round arch leaving a D-shaped tympanum between the two. Some of these are plain and others have simple diapering, star, fishscale, or lozenge patterns. From about the 1140s biblical scenes and figures appear, such as the Tree of Life at Dowdeswell, Lower Swell and Stratton, St Michael fighting a dragon at Harnhill, a Coronation of the Virgin at Quenington, and Christ in Majesty with either supporting angels or the four evangelists at Eastleach Turville, Elkstone and Little Barrington. Many Norman chancel arches survive in the Cotswolds, often adorned with one or more orders of chevrons (a continuous V-motif), another common feature of the doorways. Towards the end of the Norman period chevrons and lozenges were sometimes used in the other plane under the soffits of arches so that the points of the Vs face towards the viewer. Ozleworth has an arch of c1200-10 with undercut and pierced chevrons. In several cases the chancel arch itself is pointed and clearly a 13th or 14th century replacement set upon Norman or even Saxon jambs.

Shipton Solers Church

Alstone Church

Only a few churches had a tower before the year 1200. Those at Brockworth, Coln St Denis, Dymock, Elkstone, Great Rissington, Hampnett, South Cerney, and Withington had or have a Norman central tower between the nave and chancel. Towers at the west ends of naves had been begun at Beverston, Chedworth, Duntisbourne Abbots and North Cerney by the end of the Norman period. The early or mid 12th century towers at Ozleworth and Swindon are unique in the British Isles in being hexagonal. Both are small churches with the hexagons irregularly laid out, and originally may have consisted of just the tower to contain the congregation and an apse or tiny chancel to contain an altar, so that they would in effect have been similar in function to the circular naves of the castle chapel at Ludlow in Shropshire and Orphir Church in Orkney, themselves related to a small series of churches built by the Knights Templar and Knights Hospitaller which had ambulatories surrounding circular naves, as at Holy Sepulchre Church in Jerusalem. Another rarities which may be mentioned here are the vaulted crypt chapel below the chancel set on a sloping site at Duntisbourne Rouse, a hint of a former five-sided apse with external arcading at Dymock and the vaulted chancels at Elkstone, Hampnett, Kempley and Rudford. Kempley also has rare 12th century wall paintings and roof timbers. The churches of Baunton, Brimpsfield, Cold Aston, Notgrove and Winstone have no east window in their chancels. These are all Norman in origin, alhough the Baunton and Winstone chancels have been rebuilt.

From about the middle of the 12th century a few of the churches were enlarged by the addition of a narrow lean-to aisle, most usually on the north side if the south doorway was that most commonly used. Between the aisle and the nave would be an arcade of round arches supported on sturdy circular piers modelled on those of the abbey churches at Gloucester, Tewkesbury (and vanished Winchcombe). Early piers have square abaci. Later on the abaci are circular and the capitals have trumpet scallops, from which there was a development to crockets and then the stiff-leaf capitals of the early 13th century. Up in the Cotswold Hills congregations did not increase significantly in later centuries and many of the churches never had aisles. Of over 260 churches described in this book only a tenth of them have remains of medieval aisles on both north and south sides of the nave, the majority of these being in the towns and in large villages such as Berkeley and Slimbridge in the Vale of Severn. Just another fifty or so have a single medieval aisle, leaving over 180 churches that were aisleless at least until 18th, 19th or 20th century restoration and rebuilding.

13th century lancets in the chancel at Bibury

Work of the 13th century in the churches mainly takes the form of minor extensions, additions and rebuilding. Many chancels were lengthened and provided with stepped groups of three tall, narrow lancet windows in the east wall and single lancets and perhaps a new priest's doorway along the side walls. Examples are at Bibury, Eastleach Turville, Icomb, Little Rissington and Shipton Oliffe. Cherrington and Wyke Rissington have chancels with more ambitious east windows perhaps of c1250-75 with other openings an addition to lancets. The arrangement of two paired lancets with lozenges and angular stringcourses at Wyke Rissington is unique. Cowley is an example of a small 13th century church of west tower, nave and chancel with lancets throughout, whilst Meysey Hampton is a cruciform building with transepts, although the central tower is later, at least in its present form. Down Ampney is an aisled cruciform church mostly of c1185-1240. Still larger 13th century churches with fully aisled naves closer to the River Severn are Berkeley and Slimbridge, Berkeley having a fine west front with five stepped round-arched lancets over three pointed-arched openings with a central doorway. All three churches have later windows in the aisles and only the north aisle at Down Ampney retains a full series of lancets neither replaced nor supplimented by later windows. Pairs of 13th century arcades also remain at Deerhurst, Stow-on-the-Wold and Wotton-under-Edge. Original windows with plate tracery with round openings above paired lancets remain at Stow, especially on the north side. Teddington has a fine late 13th century window and tower arch which have come from the Cistercian abbey at Hailes, a source of several bits and pieces amongst various churches.

A number of small Cotswold churches retain 13th century bellcotes. Those at Acton Turville, Boxwell, Harescombe, and Shipton Oliffe have spirelets and pinnacles. Down Ampney has a 13th century west tower, and there are towers in a south transeptal position at Coln St Aldwyns, Oddington and Stowe-on-the-Wold, the latter later mostly rebuilt. Other south transeptal towers at Longney and Saintbury are of c1280-1320, and those at Staverton and Westonbirt are perhaps early to mid 14th century.

Work of the 14th century is unevenly spread across Gloucestershire churches. In the Cotswolds there are only odd windows, piscinae and tomb recesses inserted here and there, remodellings of older chancels, as at Meysey Hampton, and the occasional addition of a transept, aisle, chapel, porch or tower. The only mostly 14th century building is Todenham, lying in the NE corner. Closer to the River Severn there is much more to see, with a fine new set of polygonal eastern chapels and new windows and high vaults throughout the length of Tewkesbury Abbey, most of the wide-aisled cruciform church with a central spire at Cheltenham, and parts of nearby Leckhampton and Shurdington with their needle-spires. The spire at Leckhampton sits on a narrow central tower adjoining a tiny vaulted chancel. Another narrow tower with a spire is at Standish, where the exceptionally wide nave and chancel are entirely of c1340. Other notable spires of 14th century origin (even if rebuilt later) are at three parish churches in the town of Gloucester, plus those of Haresfield, Newent, Quedgeley, Slimbridge, Staunton and Stone, and on the central towers at Dowdeswell and Sapperton.

Much of the churches at Arlingham, Badgeworth, Brockworth, Bishop's Cleeve and Evenlode are 14th century, whilst Longborough and Minchinhampton have south transepts of interest, the latter vaulted with closely set buttresses on the sides. Quite a number of the churches have 13th and 14th century transepts. Twenty of the churches have pairs of medieval transepts, and another dozen churches have a single transept. They were used to contain chantry chapels and monuments, most of them being fitted with piscinae and several having tomb recesses set into the internal wall-faces

Work of the early and mid 14th centuries is in the style known as Decorated. Features of this style include window tracery with floral and net-like (reticulated) patterns and the ballflower decoration found widely in churches fairly close to the River Severn, as in the north aisle or chapel at Badgeworth and the chancel at Bishop's Cleeve. Ballflower is less common in the Cotswold churches, although it appears on the very unusual quatrefoil low-side window in the aisle at Coberley, and at South Cerney. The ogival arch was introduced c1320, appearing in the tracery of larger windows, over the heads of smaller windows, and over piscinae and the sets of triple sedilia or seats for priests commonly introduced into chancels during this period.

Evenlode Church

Doorway at Norton

The 15th century was a boom period for wool exports upon which the ecomomy of the Cotswolds was largely based. There is much work of this period in the churches of Gloucestershire. Much of it again takes the form of additions and alterations to older buildings but the chief trading centres of the wool trade have magnificent churches which result from almost complete rebuilding during this period. Those at Cirencester, Chipping Campden and Fairford contain a few older parts, whilst those of Lechlade, Northleach and Winchcombe are essentially all of the late medieval period. All six have aisled naves and chancels flanked by chapels. Winchcombe has an undivided interior without a chancel arch. Fairford has a central tower on an older set of crossing arches and the other five have western towers, that at Lechlade having a spire. Cirencester is rather bigger than the other churches, having a chapel flanking much of the north aisle of the nave, and an outer chapel beyond the north chapel of the chancel.

Sudeley has a smaller complete church of the 1460s with a turret perched on the west gable rather than a true tower, and Didbrook is also mostly late medieval, the tower there being within the west end of the nave, a layout also found at Coln Rogers and Upper Slaughter, where the towers are insertions into much older naves. Buildings still retaining some of their Norman framework but converted into late medieval glasshouses with inserted lower windows and added clerestories are Bledington, where many windows have image niches, and Chedworth. Much of the churches at Aldsworth and Bagendon and St Mary de Crypt at Gloucester are also late medieval. The porch at Aldsworth has a niche in the east wall, possibly for a rererdos for an altar. This feature is found in many porches in the Cotswolds. Bledington has a tiny chantry chapel serving also as a squint passage between the south aisle and chancel. Other chantries enclosed only by screens survive at Cirencester and Tewkesbury. Several churches have squint passages to allow the main altar to be seen from beside subsidiary altars, as at Beverston and Sevenhampton, and in others squints have been opened later on one or both sides of a narrow early chancel arch.

Wotton-under-Edge Church

Doorway at Farmcote

Work of the later medieval period is in the style known as Perpendicular because of its vertical emphasis with mullions continuing up into the arches of windows and blank panelling. This style was in vogue in England from the late 14th century through to the time of the Reformation of the 1540s. In Gloucestershire the style was introduced as early as the 1330s in the south transept of Gloucester Abbey, now the oldest extant example with the loss of some contemporary buildings in and around London. Although the Black Death caused a lull in building work generally for a couple of decades, by the 1370s towers and occasional windows in this style were being added to local parish churches and there are several which could be either late 14th or early 15th century. In Gloucester the blank panelling of the upper parts of the abbey central tower of c1450 was copied in the towers of St Michael and St Nicholas nearby. An earlier example is the upper part of the Wotton-under-Edge tower probably of the 1370s on an older base. Later medieval towers in Gloucestershire almost always have diagonal corner buttresses, often with the stringcourses carried round them. Examples are Elmstone Hardwicke, Leigh, Oxenton, and Whitminster, and the central tower at Kempsford. The lonely church at Upleadon has an unusual timber-framed tower of c1500.

Eastington and Rendcomb have fine south aisles of c1515-20, and there is a tower of about that time at Pauntley. Also of this period are the nave arcades at Cirencester and the great south porch (the largest in Britain) begun c1500. Rendcomb has the same concave sided octagonal piers that had been used along with depressed four-centred arches in the arcades of the 1450s and 80s at Northleach and Chipping Campden. These two, and Cirencester, share the rare feature of a wide window set over the chancel arch. Lechlade was given an ornate chancel roof in the early 16th century, along with a clerestory and north porch. Many Cotswold churches have fine clerestories, usually of large windows of many lights. There are plenty of later medieval roofs remaining, usually comparatively simple and plain.

Rendcomb Church

Sapperton Church   *Newent Church*

Not much building work took place in English churches between 1550 and 1700, and what there is tends to be in the nature of repairs and minor additions of a plain character. Most of the church at Naunton probably dates from the mid 16th century, there is a late 16th century chapel at Whittington and there are towers of the 1560s and c1600 respectively at Teddington and Icomb, whilst much of Dowdeswell church dates from the late 16th and early 17th centuries. The south aisle at King's Stanley is probably mid 16th century but could be as late as 1607, the date that appears on a buttress. At Alstone the north aisle and other features are of the 1620s. Great Washbourne has a chancel mostly of the 1640s and at Taynton there is a complete, but modest, new church of the 1650s built to replace one wrecked during the Civil War. The huge tower at Temple Guiting is probably late 17th century. Newent has a wide new nave of the 1670s equivilant in width to the recently collapsed medieval nave and its aisle.

The 18th century saw a spate of rebuilding of towers which had collapsed, starting in 1700 with that of Bishop's Cleeve, where the Norman arcades were also remodelled either then or earlier in the 17th century. Dursley and Somerford Keynes have towers of c1707-9, Blockley one of 1725-7, and Redmarley D'Abitot one of 1738. There is another of 1750-2 at Great Witcombe with a matching south porch, and yet another of 1750-3 at Berkeley, which is detached. All these are in the medieval style, although somewhat debased in some examples. Also Gothic in style is the large hall-church at Tetbury of 1776-81. Buildings in the new Classical style are the tower at Bourton-on-the-Water, much of the church at Hawling, that of St John the Baptist in Gloucester, small and much altered churches at Kingswood and Poole Keynes, and parts of the churches at Bromsberrow, Chalford, Sapperton and Temple Guiting.

Between the 1820s and the start of the Great War in 1914 nearly every church was restored. In some cases it amounted to little more than minor repairs to the medieval structures, at others there was a total rebuilding, except perhaps for a medieval tower allowed to remain. In most cases it was somewhere inbetween, with medieval work kept where possible and some old windows and other features reset in walling that was mostly new above the foundations. In some cases old roofs have survived the rebuilding of the walls supporting them. A lot of wall paintings and furnishings and monuments were lost during these restorations, when many churches were refurnished according to the whims of the local priest or squire, yet, as the following pages will reveal a lot of interesting and fine features and furnishings have survived, and many of the small churches in the Cotswolds still retain many old furnishings of great interest.

It was the custom for the chancels of churches to be divided from the nave by a screen to emphasise the greater sanctity of the east end. This screen became known as the Rood screen from the Holy Rood or image of the crucifixion often mounted upon the top beam. Sometimes there was a loft over over this beam for the use of musicians and the performers of religious plays. Narrow stairs beside the chancel arch or in an outer wall of an aisle or chapel are often the only reminder of a former screen and loft ripped out by Puritan reformers. Late medieval chancel screens, some of them much restored, remain at Ashchurch, Coates, Cranham, Hailes, Rendcomb and Somerford Keynes. A rarer and older stone screen remains at Ampney St Mary. Many rood screens in the churches are said to have been removed on the orders of the zealous reformer John Hooper, Bishop of Gloucester from 1550 until shortly before the catholic Queen Mary had him burnt at the stake in 1555. Other old screens used to divide off chapels can be seen at Fairford, St Mary de Crypt, Gloucester, and Stanton. Three cage-type chantry chapels associated with tombs remain by the main altar at Tewkesbury and traces of other chantry chapels remain elsewhere. Other former chantries are known only from records of their foundation or of the priests associated with them. Bisley has a very rare Poor Souls Light in the churchyard, effectively an outside chantry.

Medieval pulpits rarely survive in English churches. In any case it was only after the Reformation that sermons became an important part of services. Stanton has a late 14th century wood pulpit, and there are fine 15th century stone pulpits with tracery at Cirencester, Naunton, North Cerney and Northleach, plus a few others. Elizabethan pulpits are rare, but there are a few of later date containing 16th century panels. There are more than thirty 17th century pulpits, some of them quite ornate, as at Oddington, Shipton Solers and Windrush. Pulpits of the late 17th and 18th centuries often have a tester or sounding board above them and one or two lower levels for a reader and clerk. A three-decker pulpit of this kind remains at Didmarton. Chipping Campden has a 15th century eagle lectern, one at Fairford has feet going back to the 12th century, and there are 17th century lecterns at Eastleach Turville and Meysey Hampton.

Late medieval choir stalls with hinged seats called miserichords with carved motifs remain at Duntisbourne Rouse, Southam and Tewkesbury. The vessels used during mass were rinsed out into a basin known as a piscina normally located to the south of each altar. Not many survive from before 1200 but 13th and 14th century examples are very common, plus a few of the 15th century in the larger town churches. Sedilia or seats for the priests are also common, particularly from the 14th and 15th centuries. A few churches had a recess known as an Easter Sepulchre in which an effigy of Christ was placed during the Easter period. One at Shorncote has been set into an older window embrasure, and there are others at Cold Aston and Upper Slaughter. Many churches have 17th or 18th century altar rails or altar tables and Little Washbourne has a full set of unaltered late 18th century chancel fittings. Edgeworth, Farmcote, Forthampton, Northleach, Shipton Solers and Tewkesbury still have medieval altar slabs in use, whilst other churches still have them, but now out of use.

Pulpit at North Cerney

Font outside at Leonard Stanley

15th century font at North Nibley

More than half of the churches have old fonts. Deerhurst has a very fine and rare Saxon font and there are about fifty Norman fonts. Some are plain tubs but others have splendid carved designs. One of the 1180s at Southrop has the figures of Virtues trampling over Vices under trefoiled arches. Another of the same period at Rencomb has an arcade containing figures of the apostles. A similar design with the apostles appears on the lead fonts of the 1160s at Frampton-on-Severn, Oxenhall, and Sandhurst. They were cast from the same mould, which was also used for two Forest of Dean fonts (one is now in Gloucester Cathedral) and for another at Siston in South Gloucestershire. Lead fonts are rare since they were particularly vulnerable to being melted down (eg to make bullets during the Civil War), but there are three more in Gloucestershire, at Down Hatherley, Haresfield and Slimbridge, all perhaps 17th century, although that at Haresfield could be medieval. Fonts of the period 1200-1370 are not common. Bibury has a square one of c1300 with corner shafts, there are circular ones at Ozleworth and Todenham, and there is a good early 14th century one at Longborough. Many new fonts were made in the period 1370 - 1500, from which over fifty survive in the area covered by this book. They are generally octagonal with quatrefoils on each face and stand on pedestals which often have a cusped and recessed panel on each face. Additional motifs of angels, rosettes and shields appear occasionally and there are heads on that at Northleach. Another group of a dozen or so octagonal fonts, some with dates and intials of churchwardens, date from the Restoration period of the 1660s. In a few cases the bowl, shaft or pedestal, and base of a font are of different periods.

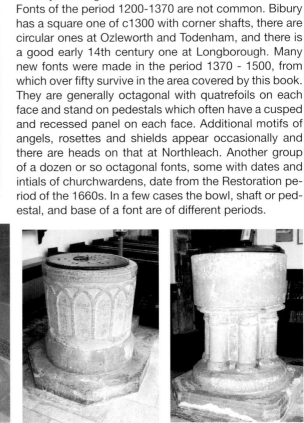

13th century font at Bibury

Norman font at Chedworth

13th century font at Hempsted

Wall painting at Baunton

Old door at Kempley

At least ten churches still have old chests in which valuables such as records and plate were kept. Medieval doors are uncommon, but sometimes older ironwork was transplanted onto a newer door. St Nicholas at Gloucester has a fine original door knocker. Old pews and benches survive in quite a number of churches, although there is nothing to compare with the fine traceried pew ends found in Devon. A few churches have some medieval floor-tiles around an altar or font. Organ cases dating from the 18th century remain at Kemble, Newent, Tewkesbury, Winchcombe and Wotton-un-der-Edge. Galleries were inserted in many churches in the 18th century, and an early 17th century musicians' gallery remains at Bishop's Cleeve, but the majority of 17th and 18th century galleries were removed by the Victorian restorers.

Medieval wall-paintings survive at Ampney Crucis, Ampney St Mary, Baunton, Beverston, Bishop's Cleeve, Bledington, Churcham, Cirencester, Duntisbourne Rouse, Fairford, Great Washbourne, Hailes, Kempley, Oddington, Shorncote, Shiton Oliffe, Stoke Orchard, Stowell, Teddington and Turkdean. A few other churches have a bit of early patterning or a fragment of a later medieval figure. Many churches eventually had fairly complete schemes showing biblical scenes but most of them were painted over during the late 16th and 17th centuries, from which period occasionally survive biblical texts or the Commandments, or a skeleton with other symbols of death, as at Salperton and Yanworth. Kempley has an unusually early and complete set of wall paintings. Many churches display the royal arms, either as a mural or painted on boards, although Henry VIII's arms appear in stone at Cirecester. Several show the arms of Queen Anne or George I and many have those of George III, so the arms of Elizabeth I at Ashchurch are a rarity, and those of Charles II at Syde are uncommon.

Fairford has an almost complete set of stained glass windows of c1500-1517, a very rare survival in a parish church. In an age when many of those attending church could not read or write the images of stained glass and wall paintings were used to convey the stories and messages contained in the Bible, although heraldry and portraits of those who paid the artists were also sometimes included. Bits of heraldic glass often survived the ravages of the Reformation when images of saints were removed. Bledington, Buckland, Cirencester, Rendcomb, and Tewkesbury have stained glass of importance, and fragments remain in the window tracery of another 35 churches.

Tomb at Mickleton

Brass at Chipping Campden

Minchinhampton: brass

About a quarter of the churches in this book contain at least one monumental effigy earlier than 1800. There are few effigies earlier than c1300 in English parish churches but Bisley has an early 13th century knight, and there are late 13th century knights at Bishop's Cleeve and Kemble, and two small female effigies at Berkeley. At Gloucester there are a knight and abbot of this period in the cathedral and a female in a hospital chapel. Effigies of the 14th century are more numerous and priests and males in civilian dress make an appearance. Coberley, Down Ampney, Frampton-on-Severn, Haresfield, Leckhampton, Longborough, Newent, Notgrove, Shipton Moyne, Tetbury, Tewkesbury, and Whittington each have two or three such effigies and there are single ones at Berkeley, Hatherop, Minchinhampton, South Cerney, Withington, and Woolstone. Many empty tomb recesses show that a lot of others have been lost. Of the 15th century are effigies at Berkeley, Ebrington, Icomb, Kempsford, and three at Tewkesbury, one of which is a cadaver. Another cadaver lies at Dursley.

Chest at Ashleworth

Including a few post-Reformation examples there are over 50 effigies of a two dimensional type with engraved lines on brass plates cut out and laid into stone slabs. There is a judge and his wife of c1400 at Deerhurst and there are collections of brasses mostly of wool-merchants at Chipping Campden and Northleach, with the finest and earliest at each again of c1400, and there are other wool-merchants at Cirencester and Fairford. There are other 15th and early 16th century brasses of note at Bisley, Blockley, Cheltenham, Dowdeswell, Eastington, Kempsford, Lechlade, Rodmarton, Sevenhampton, and Wotton-under-Edge. There are effigies in the form of flat alabaster slabs with incised lines filled with pitch at Elmore and Wormington. Twenty churches have 13th and 14th century coffin lids with incised crosses with floriated ends, with collections of them at Haresfield, Longney, Churcham, and Standish.

Elizabethan tombs often had canopies carried on columns, as at Ampney Crucis, Chipping Campden, Farmcote, Hardwicke, Sapperton and Twyning. By the early 17th century the deceased were more often shown kneeling in prayer rather than recumbent, as at Avening, Miserden, Stroud and Whitminster. A second monument at Sapperton has the common arrangement of a couple kneeling facing each other across a central prayer desk. Other good early 17th century monuments are at Broadwell, Cirencester, Down Ampney, St Nicholas at Gloucester, Shipton Moyne and Tewkesbury. By the middle of the century busts or upright half-effigies instead of full-length effigies were sometimes used, as at Ashchurch, Brockworth, Chipping Campden and Ebrington. Later on reclining effigies were fashionable, as at Blockley, Cirencester and Somerford Keynes, the latter of c1715, whilst a mid 18th century member of the Dutton family at Sherborne is depicted in Roman dress.

After the Civil Wars of the 1640s monuments increasingly took the form of tablets set upon the walls. Most of these lack figures other than cherubs or angels but they are sometimes adorned with architectural features such as columns, pediments, etc, and there may be symbols of death or symbols referring to the profession of the deceased, or even the manner of an early death. An assortment of different types of materials are sometimes used to achieve colour and contrast. Some are very fine and quite complex monuments by craftsmen based in Bristol, Bath, or the London area. Others were made more locally and vary in quality, although many have a rustic charm. Collections of 17th and 18th century tablets can be found at Alderley, Bishop's Cleeve, Blockley, Bourton-on-the Hill, Dumbleton, Eastington, Frampton-on-Severn, Haresfield, King's Stanley, Miserden, Painswick, Stroud, Tetbury, Tirley, Whittington, and Wotton-under-Edge. Most of the brasses of this period have inscriptions and sometimes heraldry and other motifs but effigies are small or absent, as in the collection of late 17th century plates at Sevenhampton. A number of churches have collections of fine ledger stones, the chancel floor at Saintbury being paved with them. Gloucestershire churchyards are noted for their fine collections of wonderfully carved 17th and 18th century tomb-chests and other monuments, particularly those of Painswick and Standish.

Part of a Dutton monument at Sherborne

Tablet at Newent

GAZETTEER OF GLOUCESTERSHIRE CHURCHES

ADLESTROP   *St Mary Magdalene*   SP 243267

The arches into the tower and chancel may be 13th century, although the embattled tower itself is 14th century. The lower stage forms a porch. The church is cruciform and has been much restored in the 18th, 19th and 20th centuries but the chancel has some medieval masonry. None of the monuments or stained slass predates the 19th century, but there are hatchments to members of the Leigh family, whose burial vault of 1774 lies outside to the south. There is a fine 15th century font with quatrefoils on the bowl and trefoil-headed niches in panels on the pedestal.

ALDERLEY   *St Kenelm*   ST 769909

In a rebuilding of c1802 a nave and north aisle were replaced by a very wide new nave to the east of which is an apsidal sanctuary. The mid 15th century NW tower is the only remaining medieval feature. The oldest of the many monuments are a tablet to Anne Workman, d1655, and others to Christopher Devonshire, d1731, William Springett, d1777, and Matthew Hale, d1784.

ALDERTON   *St Margaret*   SP 003332

The church has a south aisle with an arcade of three bays and north and south porches. Most of it is 14th century, with a piscina and credence shelf of that era in the chancel, whilst the west tower is of later on in that period. There are image niches on either side of the chancel arch and another in a north window, although most of the north wall is otherwise a rebuilding of 1890. What was once a rectangular scalloped Norman font has been altered into an octagon. There is a medieval chest with good ironwork.. On the chancel south wall is a tablet to the Reverend Henry Higford, d1795.

Alderley Church

Alderton Church

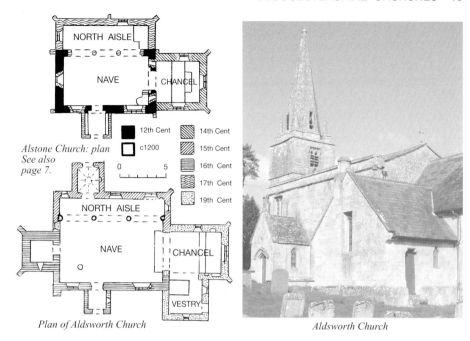

Alstone Church: plan
See also
page 7.

■ 12th Cent	▨ 14th Cent	
□ c1200	▧ 15th Cent	
	▤ 16th Cent	
	▨ 17th Cent	
	▦ 19th Cent	

Plan of Aldsworth Church

Aldsworth Church

ALDSWORTH   *St Bartholomew*   SP 154100

The three bay north arcade of c1180-1200 has two orders of chamfered pointed arches on round piers with scalloped capitals. The aisle itself was sumptuously rebuilt c1500, keeping the original width, and a rib-vaulted porch added. The outer door is dated 1636 and has a stoup beside it, whilst the inner door has old ironwork and is set in a roll-moulded inner doorway of the same period as the arcade. The east wall of the porch has a niche with a pierced stone cresset to hold lights and a tiny flue to let smoke escape. The aisle also has a fancy niche with a double canopy with shields on the frame having the initials of St Catherine. The windows have wide external splays and roll-mouldings and one has a shield over it with arms of the Abbey of Osney. There are heads around the wall-plate below the plain parapet and a fine niche on the NE buttress. The south wall of the nave also has late medieval windows and another porch with some old glass in its east window, whilst the clerestory and west tower with its spire are 16th century. There are no old furnishings, and the chancel, chancel arch and vestry date from a rebuilding of c1877.

ALSTONE   *St Margaret*   SO 983324

The Norman south doorway has shafts with scalloped capitals, a plain tympanum over a band of dog-tooth ornament, chevrons on the arch and pellets on the hood-mould. The chancel arch has similar shafts, but the pointed arch and the squints on either side are later. There is also a Norman piscina. The chancel has two trefoil-headed east lancets but the other windows may be of c1621, the date that appears on the south porch. One contains fragments of old glass. The north arcade of three bays is 15th century. There is a central wooden bell-turret. The octagonal font is 14th century. The pulpit has early 16th century linenfold panels and there are 17th century bench ends.

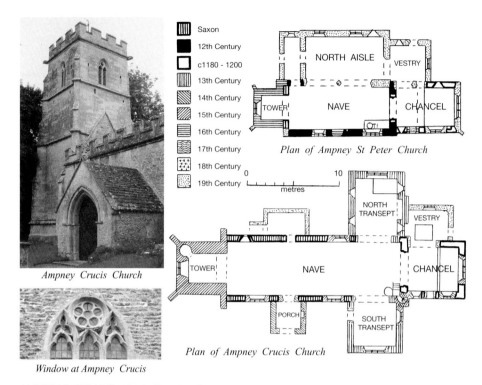

Saxon

12th Century

c1180 - 1200

13th Century

14th Century

15th Century

16th Century

17th Century

18th Century

19th Century

Plan of Ampney St Peter Church

Ampney Crucis Church

Plan of Ampney Crucis Church

Window at Ampney Crucis

AMPNEY CRUCIS *Holy Rood*   SP 154110

A heating chamber on the north side hides the exterior of a tall, narrow Saxon doorway covered with two lintels. On either side of it are Early Norman windows, one of them now blocked. The chancel has a Norman pillar-piscina and the chancel arch is Late Norman with chevrons. Transepts with lancet windows with cusped rere-arches were added in the late 13th century, the north transept still retaining an original piscina and credence shelf. Both the chancel and south transept have 15th century east windows. The north transept end window and one in the chancel south wall are 14th century. Of the 15th century are the bellcote on the nave east gable, windows on either side of the nave, the eastern niche of the 13th century south porch, and the ashlar-faced west tower with diagonal buttresses.

Many wall-paintings were revealed during a restoration in 1870. Figures of saints and the Fitzhamon arms remain in the north transept and under the tower is a copy of a former painting of the martyrdom of St Erasmus. The Norman font has a stem of c1860, the original now being outside. There is a late medieval stone pulpit with pan-elling, and there are Jacobean pews (one dated 1618) and an altar table. The monuments include recumbent effigies of George Lloyd, d1584, and his wife on a tomb chest under a pedimented canopy, a marble monument to Robert Playdell, d1719, a series of other tablets to 17th century members of the Playdell family in the south transept, and a vase, pyramid and cherub heads to John Radway, d1784. The head of the churchyard cross is carved with a knight of c1415, St Laurence with his gridiron, the Virgin Mary, and the Crucifixion.

Lintel at Ampney St Mary

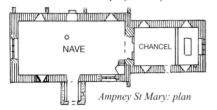

Ampney St Mary: plan

East window, Ampney St Mary

AMPNEY ST MARY *St Mary* SP 075015

The nave SW window may be Saxon and is a small opening pierced through a single stone with an external rebate for a shutter (see page 5). The internal rebate was perhaps intended for an openable frame with an animal skin instead of glass. The nave is otherwise early 12th century and has a north doorway lintel with the Lion of Righteousness in triumph over snake-like agents of the devil, who are assisted by a griffon. In the 13th century the chancel was extended and given two lancets on the north side and a stepped triple lancet on the east, whilst the south side has a priest's doorway with a shouldered arch, and part of a plain original stone screen also remains. Of the 14th century are the chancel and the bellcote over it, the three-light west window, the wagon roofs and the south doorway, complete with its door. The only 15th century features are one window incorporating a piscina on the south side of the nave and a niche in the east wall of the porch which incorporates a re-used 12th century grave-slab.

The church has a fine series of old wall-paintings. The chancel north wall has a painted ashlar stone effect with cinquefoils and tendrils. In the nave are St Christopher, St George and the Dragon, part of a rich canopy, and on the south wall is a 14th century mural of the commandment "Keep Holy the Sabbath Day". It shows that labour on Sunday wounds Christ, his wounds being shown, along with the implements of manual labour that inflicted them. The altar table and communion rails are 17th century and the font adorned with a chevron band is 12th century.

AMPNEY ST PETER *St Peter* SP 082015

The round-headed tower arch of through stones is evidence that the nave is Late Saxon. The tower itself is small and low, and is late medieval. The Late Norman chancel arch has a billeted hood-mould. In 1878 Sir George Gilbert Scott restored the church and added a new north aisle with a porch west of it. Two small original lancets were reset, one of them in the new NE vestry. Of the 15th century are the octagonal font, the rood-loft staircase in the nave NE corner, the double piscina with a credence shelf in the nave SE corner and one south window. Another south window is 16th century. There is a 14th century churchyard cross. See picture on page 22.

Arlingham Church

ARLINGHAM   *St Mary*   SO 706107

The church is mostly 14th century and has a
south porch and a diagonally buttressed west
tower with an open panelled parapet. The
chancel has reticulated tracery in the east window and a piscina and a credence shelf with
a cinquefoiled head. The octagonal font has a
panelled stem. Two windows in the nave north
wall have stained glass of c1340 depicting
several saints, including St Catherine with her
wheel, whilst a chancel window has restored
15th century glass. The pulpit and the almsbox
are probably early 18th century. There are also
two chandeliers made in Bristol in 1772.

Ampney St Peter Church

ASHCHURCH   *St Nicholas*   SO 928334

The long nave has a Norman south wall with one window with cable-moulding and the
outer order of a doorway with chevrons. A new chancel the same width as the nave
was provided in the 13th century and later in that century a north aisle was added with
a six bay arcade. The diagonally-buttressed west tower with panelled and crocketted pinnacles is late 14th century. Also of that period is the inner order of the south
doorway and the two storey porch in front of it. The clerestory and embattled parapet
are late 15th or early 16th century. There are old roofs, the chapel at the east end of
the aisle having portraits and initials on a frieze at wall-plate level. The font has a 16th
century bowl on a 16th century base. The medieval rood screen survives in a much
restored state and there is a screen made of 17th century panelling below the organ.
There are royal arms of George I. There is a bust of William Ferrers, d1625, and also a
brass to Robert Barker, d1671.

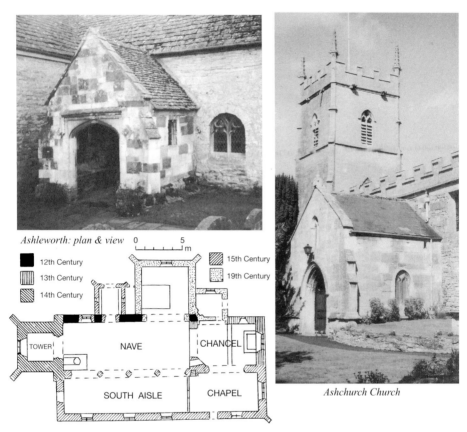

Ashleworth: plan & view   0   5 m

■ 12th Century
▥ 13th Century
▨ 14th Century

▨ 15th Century
▦ 19th Century

TOWER   NAVE   CHANCEL

SOUTH AISLE   CHAPEL

Ashchurch Church

ASHLEWORTH   *St Andrew & St Bartholomew*   SO 819252

Part of the nave north wall has Early Norman herringbone masonry with the outlines of a window and doorway. A 19th century vestry now obscures a group of three lancets in the north wall of the 13th century chancel. The diagonally buttressed west tower has gargoyles at the top and a spire. The south aisle was added in the mid 15th century and then a south chapel was provided, with a single arch to the chancel in line with the arcade, thus widening the chancel, which was given a new east window, and a squint beside the chancel arch. In the chapel, which has a restored original screen, are a piscina with ballflowers and a priest's doorway which are 14th century work reset. The east end of the aisle has a boarded roof with ribs and bosses, the other roofs having trussed rafters with curved struts and moulded tiebeams. At the west end of the aisle are royal arms of Elizabeth I on boards once fixed over the chapel screen and originally probably painted with a Doom scene. A few of the benches have 16th century linenfold panels. Of the early 17th century are the altar table, altar rails, pulpit and reading desk dated 1635. One south window has fragments of old glass and there is an old chest. The churchyard cross with figures of St Mary and St John and a crucifixion scene is late 14th century. Near the church is a fine tithe barn of c1500 which served the abbey of St Augustine at Bristol, which was the patron of the church from 1154 onwards.

Ashley Church

ASHLEY *St James*   ST 931948

The chancel and the nave north wall were rebuilt during the restoration by F.S. Waller in 1858. The chancel arch is Early Norman work of c1100 and the south doorway with a lintel and tympanum with dogtooth and hoseshoe-diapering and one order of shafts is not much later. The narrow south aisle of c1200 has piers with clustered shafts and foliated capitals. One window was made in the 17th century from a 13th century coffin-lid. The west tower has an embattled 15th century upper stage. There is a 17th century monument of coloured stone and brass to Ann Hauers, and there is a painted stone to Ferdinando Gorges, d1718. The 14th century font lies on a 19th century base.

ASTON SUB EDGE *St Andrew*   SP 139417

The church of 1797 is just a small nave with a polygonal apse. The windows may be later but the font, west gallery and pulpit could all be of the 1790s.

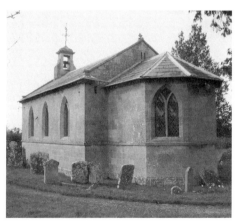

Aston sub Edge Church

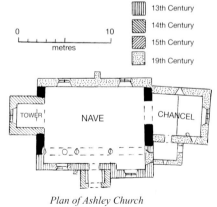

	12th Century
	13th Century
	14th Century
	15th Century
	19th Century

0 — 10
metres

Plan of Ashley Church

Avening: main entrance

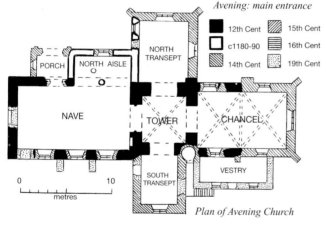

■ 12th Cent		▨ 15th Cent	
□ c1180-90		▤ 16th Cent	
▨ 14th Cent		▦ 19th Cent	

Plan of Avening Church

Avening Church

AVENING   *Holy Cross*   ST 880980

The nave, central tower and the western part of the chancel are all Early Norman but the transepts are mostly 14th century, as is the eastern part of the chancel, with a piscina and east window of that date. Both parts of the chancel and the crossing have rib-vaults and Norman windows remain in the crossing and west part of the chancel. There is a narrow north aisle with a two bay Late Norman arcade. Further west is a Norman north doorway in which is set a 16th century doorway with leaf spandrels. On either side of it are Norman sculptured panels. These are all enclosed within a two storey porch of c1300. The north transept has restored 14th century windows. The west arch of the crossing is a pointed later insertion on the original jambs with carved heads. To the south of it is a nave altar with an old piscina and an altar table of 1657. There are many 17th, 18th and 19th century memorial tablets, plus a kneeling effigy of the pirate Henry Brydges, d1615 in the north transept, whilst the south transept has a rustic collection of Baroque monuments to the Driver family.

BADGEWORTH   *Holy Trinity*   SO 901192

The consecration recorded in 1315 seems to refer to the addition of the chapel or aisle on the north side of the nave with a three bay arcade, and windows adorned with ballflowers containing fragments of old glass. The wagon roofs with ribs and bosses are also 14th century. The church served a cell of the Benedictine priory of Usk. The south porch and the chancel were rebuilt in 1869, although the east window is original. The west tower is late 14th or early 15th century. The pulpit incorporates 16th century linenfold panels. The step of the south doorway is a reused coffin lid with an incised foliated cross. The monuments include those of William Hynson, d1667, Sara Gwinnett, d1717, and George Gwinnett Gough, d1756.

BAGENDON   *St Margaret*   SP 011067

The thin walls of the nave could be partly Saxon, or at least on Saxon foundations, and there are Early Norman openings pierced through single stones reset in the diagonally buttressed west tower. The second stage formed a habitable room for a priest with an east window looking into the church. The three bay north arcade with arches of two chamfered orders upon round piers is Late Norman. A chantry chapel was later formed within the aisle and the floor level of this and the chancel were raised so alleviate the effects of occasional flooding. In the south wall is one 14th century window. In the 1460s the Weavers' Guild at Cirencester had the chancel rebuilt, and it has windows with fragments of glass of that period. The capital on the south side of the chancel arch then inserted in place of the very narrow original one was removed in the 18th century to allow room for the sounding-board of a pulpit. The tower arch is of 1830 and a new south porch of that period was rebuilt again in 1962. The font and three coffin lids around the tower and porch are Norman. The altar table is 17th century. There are tablets to William Huntingdon, d1737, and Ralph Oliffe, d1762.

Bagendon Church

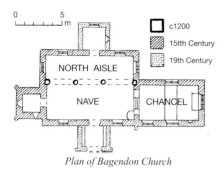

Plan of Bagendon Church

Badgeworth Church

BARNSLEY *St Mary* SP 077052

The chancel retains a Norman corbel table with grotesque heads, and there is a 13th century chancel arch set upon leaning Norman piers with shafts with scalloped capitals with large pellets on the abaci. The roll-moulded north doorway is also Norman. A small Norman window in the organ chamber and a 13th century window in the nave were moved here from Daglingworth. The chancel has a restored 13th century piscina, an aumbry with wooden lining, and restored windows and a trussed-rafter roof of the 14th century. The north porch with an eastern altar niche and the north aisle with its two bay arcade are late 15th century work sponsored by Sir Edmund Tame of Fairford. The tower is also of that period, and has original glass in the west window, although the upper stage is of c1600, and has finials on the four gables. A restoration of 1843-7 removed all traces of an 18th century remodelling in which the roofs were provided with ceilings and several new windows inserted. The altar-table is of c1580-1620. The monuments include tablets of Elizabeth Bourchier, d1691, Sarah Bourchier, d1762, and several interesting ledger stones in the nave.

Norman features at Barnsley Church

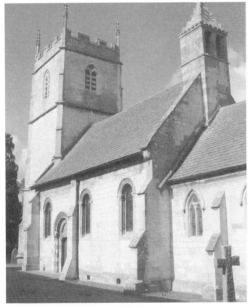

Barnwood Church

Berkeley Church

BARNWOOD   *St Lawrence*   SO 859178

The nave is Norman but its features are mostly 19th century restorations, although some original work remains in the north doorway. The arcade piers are Norman but the chamfered pointed arches are later. Over the east gable of the nave is a 14th century bellcote with an ogee crocketed canopy. The diagonally buttressed 16th century west tower has in a spandel of its west doorway the arms of Abbot Parker, last abbot of Gloucester Abbey. The octagonal font with winged angels holding shields and a chamfered stem with niches, and also the north chapel with with an original moulded roof, appear to be of the same period. There are tablets to Beata Johnson, d1722, Elizabeth Whitehead, d1750, and Thomas Parker, d1800.

BATSFORD   *St Mary*   SP 188339

The church itself was rebuilt in 1861-2 but there are two older monuments, one a coloured marble tablet of the 1750s to Richard Freeman, and the other to Elizabeth Freeman, d1781.

BAUNTON   *St Mary Magdalene*   SP 022047

The chancel is entered through a Norman arch and has no east window. Part of the late medieval screen now forms part of a reredos. The nave has a restored late 13th century north window with plate tracery and a west window of the 14th century. Also 14th century is the huge wall painting on the north wall showing St Christopher carrying the Child Jesus through a stream full of fish. The landscape behind has trees, churches and a windmill. The nave south window and parapet are 15th century, and also of that period is the altar frontal in a case. Set on the original Norman font bowl is a polygonal early 16th century bowl. The pulpit has been made up from Jacobean parts. See p15.

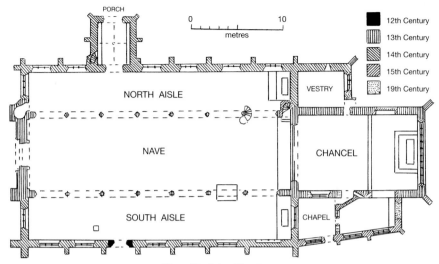

Plan of Berkeley Church

BERKELEY *St Mary* ST 861940

The churchyard formed part of the outer defences of the adjacent castle, which is why there is a detached tower to the north, where it could not menace the castle garrison if captured. It is now a structure of the 1750s on a 15th century base. Originally there was a Saxon minster here. The church had ten chaplains serving it in 1338, and had three chantry chapels at the time of the Reformation. The only Norman parts are the reset south doorway, the rectangular font with scallops and corner shafts. and a pillar piscina now at the west end. Of c1225-50 are the seven bay arcades with piers with filleted shafts and stiff-leaf capitals, the south clerestory, the fine west front with five steeped round-headed lancets, and part of the chancel with one north lancet. Much of the interior has late 13th century red patterned wall-paintings and there is a fragment of a Doom scene over the chancel arch. In the 14th century the aisles were rebuilt with windows of three steeped cinquefoil-headed lights between buttresses without set-offs, a vaulted north porch added (it has an original door), and the chancel given an Easter Sepulcre recess on the north side. The chancel was remodelled in the 15th century with new east and south windows, a vaulted south chapel added, and an upper chamber added to the porch. Also 15th century are the fine stone screen with a staircase on the north side, and the roofs.

In the Berkeley Chapel are alabaster recumbent effigies of James, 11th Lord Berkeley, d1463, and his second son James. They have Yorkist collars of suns and roses. On a tomb chest are effigies of Henry, 17th Lord Berkeley, d1615 and his wife. On a tomb chest in the nave are recumbent effigies of Thomas, 8th Lord Berkeley, d1361 and his wife. Thomas had custody of the captive Edward II when he was murdered in 1327. The two small 13th century female effigies and a similar 14th century one of a male in civilian dress probably represent heart burials of members of the Berkeley family buried in St Augustine's abbey at Bristol. Other monuments include a brass to William Freme, d1526, ledger stones of John Hopton, d1681 and Stephen Jenner, d1754, and tablets to James Bayley, d1712, Betty Wiltshire, d1797, and Nicholas Hickes, d1798.

Beverston Church

Arcade in Bibury Church

BEVERSTON   *St Mary*   ST 861940

The tower has a late medieval embattled and pinnacled top on an Early Norman lower stage. Set upon the south face is a Saxon depiction of the Resurrection. The chancel was rebuilt in the 14th century and has a chancel-arch, a good east window and a corner piscina of that period, but in the north wall are a Norman window and another of the 13th century. The nave south doorway is Norman and has crocket capitals on the shafts and inverted crockets on the hood-mould of the round arch. The south arcade of three pointed arches on circular piers with stiffleaf and trumpet-scallop capitals is 13th century. There were formerly traces of wall paintings in the 15th century north transept or Berkeley Chapel. It has squint passage towards the chancel. There is a stone 16th century pulpit, and an old font which appears to have been recut. Four cof-fin-lids with incised foliated crosses are set on the north wall of the nave and the west wall of the chapel. Other monuments of note are a brass to Elizabeth Brydges, d1693 set in tomb recess in the south aisle, and a tablet to William Tugwell, d1763.

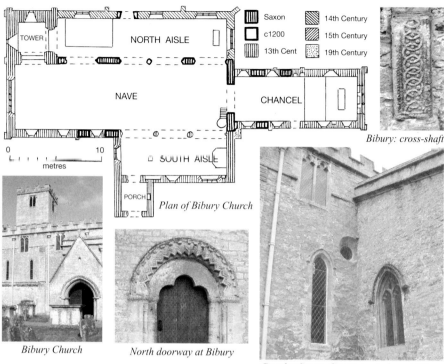

Saxon
c1200
13th Cent
14th Century
15th Century
19th Century

TOWER

NORTH AISLE

NAVE

CHANCEL

0   10
metres

SOUTH AISLE

PORCH

Plan of Bibury Church

Bibury: cross-shaft

Bibury Church

North doorway at Bibury

Circular Saxon clerestory window at Bibury

BIBURY   *St Mary*   SP 118065

Of a large and important Saxon church here there remain parts of the nave walls with pilaster strips visible above the Norman arches into the north aisle and a circular clerestory window on the south, the imposts of the chancel arch with foliage on the north side, and the west part of the chancel with a pilaster strip still remaining on each side. On the chancel north wall is reset part of a Saxon cross-shaft and there are two casts of 11th century grave-slabs, the originals now being in the British Museum. The tower at the west end of the aisle is early 13th century, and the nave west wall may be contemporary. There are also two 13th century lancets set in Saxon walling at the west end of the south wall. The north doorway of c1200 has a trefoiled head, possibly cut into an earlier plain tympanum and the shafts have abaci with ribbed leaves. The round-arched south doorway with dogtooth on the hoodmould and the south porch are of c1200-20. There are several 14th century north windows. Most of the chancel is 13th century and it has many aumbries. One lancet on each side is carried down as a low-side window and has marks of a former grille. There are triple-stepped east lancets, arcaded both inside and out. The small SE window with old glass probably lighted a sacristy tucked in between the east wall and the high altar. The tower top is 15th century, and also of that date are the clerestory windows under an embattled parapet, the nave ceiling, and the west windows of the nave and south aisle. See p8.

The 12th century font (see p14) has panels of pointed arches, four corner shafts and a central pier. The monuments include 17th and 18th century ledger stones to the Coxwells of Ablington, brass inscriptions to Edith Lambert, d1702, and John Matthews, d1707, and tablets to Anne Cresswell, d1756, and Katharine Sackville, d1760.

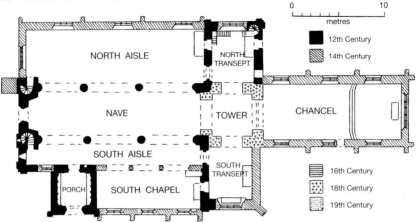

■	12th Century
▨	14th Century
▤	16th Century
▦	18th Century
▨	19th Century

Plan of Bishop's Cleeve Church

BISHOP'S CLEEVE   *St Michael*   SO 961278

Of a fine Late Norman cruciform church there remain the north transept, the south transept west window containing later stained glass, the west front with a splendid doorway with chevrons and a pair of square stair-turrets, and the south porch containing another splendid doorway. The arcades were originally of six bays but in a 17th century rebuilding alternate piers were removed and new arches provided. In the 14th century the south transept was mostly rebuilt, a splendid new west window inserted in the nave, the north aisle rebuilt much wider than beforehand, and a long new chancel provided with pellets in the eaves course and ballflowers on the priest's doorway and the east window. More ballflowers occur on a tomb recess in the south transept which is cinquefoiled with triple cusps. A chapel was inserted between the south transept and the porch. It has 16th century windows. The central tower was rebuilt in 1700 after the original collapsed in 1696.

Bishop's Cleeve Church

Both transepts have remains of wall-paintings and slight remains survive of a scene of St Christopher on the north aisle north wall. The font is Elizabethan and the pulpit and west gallery are 17th century. The log chest has Norman locks. In the south transept is an effigy of a knight of c1270. A female effigy of c1500 in the south chapel has winged angels beside the head. Also in the south chapel is an elaborate monument with recumbent effigies of Richard de la Bere, d1636 and his wife. The many tablets include those of Edmund Bedingfield, d1695, Catherine Norwood, d1711, Thomas Beale, d1782, and Mary Smith, d1787.

Tomb recess at Bisley

BISLEY *All Saints* SO 904060

Much of the exterior of the church was re-stored in 1862 and the piers of the arcades appear to be Victorian, but with original bases and capitals of the 13th century on the south side and of the 14th century on the north side. The only Norman relic is a font with basket-work, a cable moulding and fleur-de-lys set on a stem of the 1860s. A tomb recess on the south side is the only relic of a chantry chapel here which existed in 1274. A conse-cration recorded in 1315 probably dates the chancel. One of its cinquefoil-headed north lancets is now blocked by a vestry. Reset in the roof of this vestry, and also in the 14th century west tower, are carvings of musicians playing recorders and bagpipes from the former 15th century roof of the nave. There are double piscinae in the chancel, in the NE corner of the nave, and also near the south doorway. There are royal arms of George III. In the south aisle is an early 13th century ef-figy of a knight on a tomb chest. There are several 18th century tablets under the tower and there is a brass depicting Kateryn Sewell, d1515. The poor souls' light in the church-yard is the only English example outside of a church. It is hexagonal on a circular base and has trefoil-headed arches supporting a spire with trefoil-headed gable openings.

Bisley: poor souls light

West front at Bishop's Cleeve

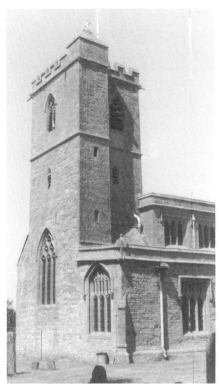

Bledington Church

Bledington Church

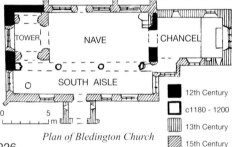

Plan of Bledington Church

TOWER | NAVE | CHANCEL

SOUTH AISLE

0   5
|_____|m

■ 12th Century

☐ c1180 - 1200

▥ 13th Century

▨ 15th Century

BLEDINGTON   *St Leonard*   SP 245226

The east and west walls still remain of the Norman nave, although the bellcote over the plain chancel arch has probably been transferred from the west gable when a tower was built on three arches set within the nave. The arcade remains of a south aisle added c1200 and then a few years later the porch was added and the chancel was extended and given a set of three stepped east lancets. Near them is a trefoil-headed piscina. The west window is 14th century, which is also the likely period of the cusped recess which provided a reredos for a nave altar beside the chancel arch. In the 15th century the building was remodelled at the expense of Winchcombe Abbey. It was given fine new windows fitted internally with pedestals and canopies for niches, a clerestory and a new roof. The windows retain parts of their original stained glass with the date 1470, the maker probably being John Prudde of Westminster. Depicted are St Christopher, St Mary, St George and the Dragon, St Mary Magdalene, the Pieta and a group of donors. Traces of patterned 13th century wall paintings remain near the chancel arch. Old furnishings include a Norman tub-font, an hourglass stand, the Jacobean altar table and communion rail, and some old bench ends.

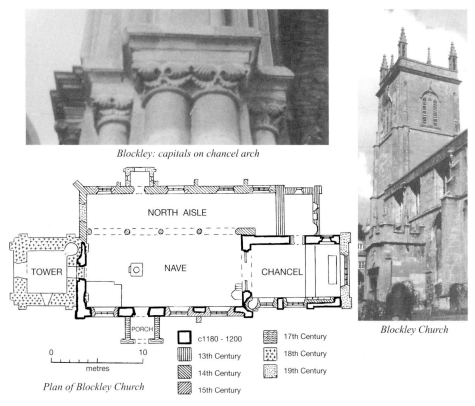

Blockley: capitals on chancel arch

NORTH AISLE

TOWER

NAVE

CHANCEL

PORCH

0 ___ 10
metres

□ c1180 - 1200
▥ 13th Century
▧ 14th Century
▨ 15th Century
▒ 17th Century
▦ 18th Century
░ 19th Century

Blockley Church

Plan of Blockley Church

BLOCKLEY   *St Peter & St Paul*   SP 165350

The three bay Late Norman chancel has shafts for intended vaulting and one original unaltered window with internal and external shafts. Two others are now blocked and others on the south side were modified in the 14th century, when the piscina and sedilia were provided. The corbel table has pairs of arches and pendant-brackets between the corbels. The fine chancel arch is pointed and has ribbed leaves and scallops on the shafts. The east wall was rebuilt in 1838. A two storey chapel, now the vestry, was added on the north side after 1270, when Blockley became a prebend for the college founded by Bishop Giffard of Worcester at Westbury-on-Trym. The nave has Norman doorways facing west and south, one blocked by a medieval-looking tower actually of 1725-27, and the other with a later medieval arch inserted below it. The north arcade lies beyond where the original north wall lay. The clerestory is dated 1636 and the look of the capitals suggests that just before then the arcade was rebuilt, using 14th century materials. The south porch is also of c1630. The north porch dates from the restoration of 1871. A brass shows Philip Neele, d1510, kneeling in full mass vestments (very rare), and another depicts Philip Warthim, d1485, in a cope. There are also kneeling effigies of William Childe and his wife, d1633, and of William Childe, d1615, a reclining marble effigy of Anne Mary Childe, d1659, and tablets to Edward Carter, 1667, Sir James Rushout, d1711, Edward Croft, 1717, Erasmus Saunders, d1771, the Reverend Charles Selwyn, d1794, and other members of the Rushout family.

Boddington Church

Font at Brimpsfield

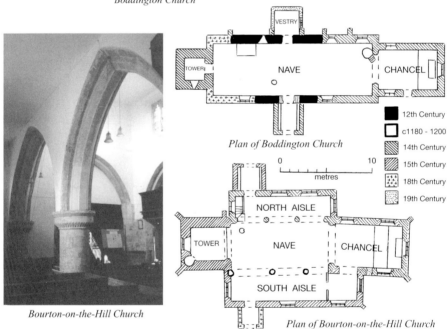

Bourton-on-the-Hill Church

Plan of Boddington Church

	12th Century
	c1180 - 1200
	14th Century
	15th Century
	18th Century
	19th Century

Plan of Bourton-on-the-Hill Church

BODDINGTON   *St Mary Magdalene*   SO 895252

The long Norman nave has one original window and a north doorway now leading into a vestry. Several of the windows and the roof and south porch are 14th century. The walls are set on unstable clay foundations and have needed heavy buttressing on the north side. The truncated and pyramidal-roofed west tower bearing a sundial of 1719 and the south doorway are 13th century. The chancel was heavily restored in 1876. The chest is of 1676, the altar-rails are 17th century and there is late medieval font.

BOURTON-ON-THE-HILL   *St Laurence*   SP 175326

The south arcade has Norman piers but the pointed arches are later. One arch seems to have been shortened when a new chancel was built in the 14th century, along with a north aisle with an arcade of hexagonal piers. The west tower is late 14th century or early 15th century. The exterior was transformed in the 15th century with the addition of a clerestory and parapets with fine gargoyles, a north porch, the rebuilding of the south aisle, and the insertion of a window in the chancel north wall. The south porch is 18th century. In the south aisle are remains of a stone screen said to have come from Morton-in-Marsh. The octagonal font is 15th century and a north gallery of c1780 has managed to survive the alterations to the seating in 1893. The best of several 18th century tablets in the south aisle is that of Ann Batson, d1763.

BOURTON-ON-THE-WATER   *St Lawrence*   SP 167209

The original Norman nave and central tower were replaced in the 1780s, leaving just the chancel of the 1320s. The Georgian tower dated 1785 with a lead-covered dome was allowed to remain when there was another rebuilding of the nave in the mid 19th century. A north aisle was added in 1875 and a south porch in 1890. The chancel retains several medieval windows, with sedilia set into one of them, and a piscina alongside. It has a 19th century roof which was superbly painted in 1928. The many monuments include those of Anthony Collett, d1719 and George Vernon, d1720. Outside in the churchyard are a medieval coffin with sloping sides and a rectangular head recess, which was found under a chantry chapel, a recumbent female effigy of c1600 and many fine table tombs and headstones of the 17th and 18th centuries.

Bourton-on-the-Hill Church   *Bourton-on-the-Water Church*

BOXWELL   *St Mary*   SO 812927

The church is mostly 13th century, with a squint flanking the narrow chancel arch. Original also are the octagonal font, the south porch and the bellcote under an octagonal spirelet. Of c1300 are the narrow north aisle with a three bay arcade with octagonal piers and the west window with cusped intersecting tracery. Royal arms of Queen Anne are painted on the wall over the chancel arch and in front of it are the communion rails of the 1630s. The monuments include those of Elizabeth Glasse, d1757, and Elizabeth Johnson, d1775.

BRIMPSFIELD   *St Michael*   SO 942128

The 15th century central tower is carried on an Early Norman chancel arch to the east and a 15th century arch on two older piers to the west. The Early Norman south doorway has a plain arch and tympanum. The chancel was rebuilt slightly longer in the 13th century and retains an original lancet on one side and a priest's doorway and square-headed double piscina on the other. There is no east window. Two south windows are 14th century and the west window is 15th century. The nave has an old roof. The squints and vestry are 19th century. The octagonal font with quatrefoils is 15th century and the pulpit is dated 1658. There is also a 12th century altar slab with four consecration crosses which was rescued from being part of a local stile in 1937. There are brass inscriptions to Humphrey Taylor, d1745 and William and Elizabeth Lawrence, d1757, and there are tablets to the Reverend William Walbank, d1784 and Humphrey Taylor, 1745. In the SW corner of the churchyard is a fine Norman stone coffin-lid carved with a large sword for one of the Giffards of the adjacent castle.

Brimpsfield Church

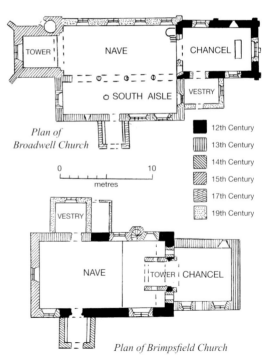

Plan of Brimpsfield Church

Broadwell Church

Monument in Broadwell Church

BROADWELL   *St Paul*   SP 200278

The lower parts of the chancel (below the stringcourse) are Norman. The nave north wall was rebuilt in 1860 and a fine tympanum with a Maltese cross has been reset into the stairwell of the late 14th or 15th century tower. Of the 13th century are the chancel arch, the south arcade of four bays and the south doorway. The squint is probably 19th century and the aisle has 14th and 17th century windows. The octagonal font with quatrefoils is early 15th century. There are kneeling alabaster effigies of Herbert Weston, d1635 and his family, and also a tablet to Robert Hunckes, d1585. In the churchyard is a fine set of early 17th century table-tombs with "wool bale" type tops.

BROCKWORTH   *St George*   SO 891170

The font bowl and the arches of three orders under the central tower date from about the time of the dedication of 1142, when the church was given to Llanthony Priory. The tower top is 19th century but most of the rest of the church is 14th century. A shallow transept with an original roof with bosses lies south of the nave between the tower and porch. The north aisle has a three bay arcade with ballflowers on the capitals of the piers. The chancel has a pillar piscina and an east window with reticulated tracery. There is a Baroque monument to Sir Christopher Guise, d1670. See page 40.

BROMSBERROW   *St Mary*   SO 743337

The nave was rebuilt when a north aisle was added in 1858. The tower has a 13th century lowest stage of stone and a timber-framed upper part mostly rebuilt in 1875, when a shingled spire was added, although the beam over the opening to the nave is dated 1502. The chancel is 14th century, but much restored. North of it is the Yate Chapel, the east window of which contains medieval and 17th century stained glass. The oldest of the monuments to the Yate family is that of John, d1749. Mounted on a shaft of 1882 is a 13th century churchyard cross. There are royal arms of George III.

Brookthorpe Church

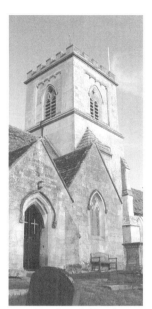

Brockworth Church

Heads on the chancel windows at Brockworth

BROOKTHORPE   *St Swithin*   SO 835123

A north aisle was added in 1892 to a mostly 13th century church with a single lancet for an east window and a saddle-back roofed west tower. The chancel arch is flanked by a recess and a rood staircase. On the cornice of the porch is a chronogram commemorating the execution of Charles I. There is a tablet to George Venn, d1694.

BUCKLAND   *St Michael*   SP 082360

The nave and narrow aisles with arcades of quatrefoil-shaped piers are 13th century. The north aisle retains east and west lancets, and both aisles have original piscinae. The west tower and the north porch are 14th century. A new set of windows and a clerestory and a flatter new roof for the nave were provided c1500. The roof has pendant bosses below kingposts. The aisles also have old roofs with carved bosses. The chancel was rebuilt in the 16th century and is dated 1585 on a panel over a domestic-looking east window containing glass of the 1470s given by Rector William Grafton which depicts some of the Seven Sacraments. The arms of Gloucester Abbey appear in other fragments of 15th century glass in a south window. Some oak benches are 15th century, and there is a west gallery and much other seating and wainscoting of the late 17th century, although an inscription suggests older parts were reused. There are 15th century stones with painted angels in panels said to be from Hailes Abbey. A 15th century cope is also associated with the abbey, as the letters WHY and a church must refer to William Whychurch, abbot from 1464 to 1479. There is a tablet to James Thynne, d1709. Outside in the churchyard are the base of a 14th century cross, a 14th century table-tomb with large quatrefoils, and an 18th century table tomb to the parents of Mrs Delany, nee Granville.

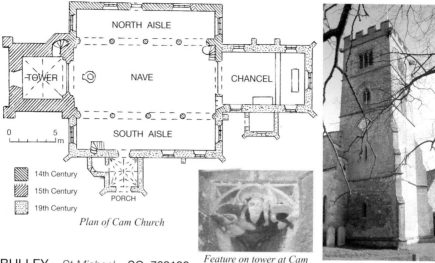

NORTH AISLE

TOWER

NAVE

CHANCEL

SOUTH AISLE

0 5
m

14th Century
15th Century
19th Century

PORCH

Plan of Cam Church

Feature on tower at Cam

Buckland Church

BULLEY *St Michael* SO 762198

The chancel of this small Norman church was rebuilt in 1886. The north windows retain original red painted chevron patterns, and there are three dimensional chevrons on the chancel arch of two orders and the south doorway with a plain tympanum. The shafts of the doorway (in which are alternating stones of different colours - blue lias and sandstone) have key patterns, leaves on the capitals and spurs on the bases. The font with a roll at the top and bottom is Norman too.

CAM *St George* ST 757994

The church was mostly rebuilt c1340 at the expense of Thomas, Lord Berkeley as a way of expressing remorse for the murder of Edward II at Berkeley Castle and the only older features are the 13th century chancel arch and font. The west tower buttresses which are diagonal set on square bases and a vaulted tower arch now containing a glass screen. The north aisle was rebuilt in the 15th century and the chancel is of 1845, when the porch and south aisle were rebuilt and a clerestory provided. The pulpit is Jacobean.

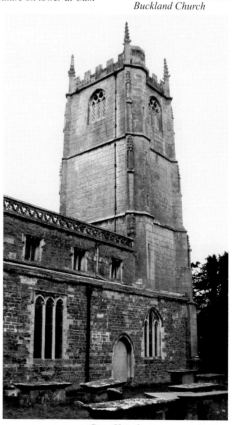

Cam Church

CHACELEY *St John the Baptist*   ST 757994

The Norman chancel arch has intersecting chevrons and a grotesque keystone under a double row of billets. The shafts have scalloped capitals. In the 14th century a new upper stage was added to the 13th century west tower and an aisle added with a four bay arcade with corbel heads of male figures on octagonal piers. The roof and the piscina with a crocketed canopy are original. The north wall has been rebuilt in brick. In the much rebuilt chancel are a cinquefoil-headed piscina, an aumbry and a few old tiles. Two windows have fragments of 14th century glass. The font is also probably 14th century and there are 15th century bench ends with carved panels. None of the tablets in the chancel predate the early 19th century.

CHALFORD   *Christ Church*   SO 892026

The nave and north aisle are of 1724 but were lengthened in 1841 when the chancel was added. The south side is mostly of 1857, when two porches were added, in addition to a west tower. The pulpit is the only pre-Victorian furnishing. See page 159.

CHARLTON ABBOTS *St Martin*   SP 034243

The church lay ruinous in the 18th century and much of it dates from a restoration in 1887. The round-headed south doorway may be late 12th century. The font bowl and two chancel lancets with trefoiled rere-arches are 13th century.

CHARLTON KINGS *St Mary*   SO 965205

The vaulted central tower and the transepts are 15th century. The south transept has an earlier piscina and indications that it was intended to be vaulted. The south wall and porch are early 16th century and the north wall is partly of 1826, but otherwise the nave and aisles and the chancel were rebuilt in 1877-78. The font appears to be a Norman tub recut into an octagon in the 14th century. The oldest of the monuments are those to Elizabeth Prinn, d1771, and John Whithorne, d1797. See picture on title page.

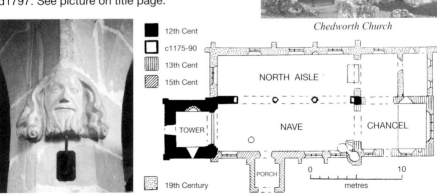

Chedworth Church

12th Cent
c1175-90
13th Cent
15th Cent

NORTH AISLE

TOWER   NAVE   CHANCEL

PORCH

0   10

metres

19th Century

Head in Chaceley Church   *Plan of Chedworth Church*

CHEDWORTH   *St Andrew*   SP 051122

The west tower and its tower arch of three orders are Late Norman, and so is the three bay north arcade with piers that are cruciform with corner shafts. The aisle itself was rebuilt in 1883. The tower top is 13th century, although the parapet is 15th century. The small chancel is 13th century and has one partly blocked north lancet and a trefoiled piscina. The porch on the south side is 13th or 14th century but otherwise the façade is 15th century work. On the buttress east of the porch is the date 1461 and an inscription mentioning Richard Sely, probably the bailiff of Richard Neville. On the stair-turret at the SE corner is the date 1485, the year in which Anne Neville's husband King Richard III was killed in the battle of Bosworth. The clerestory over the arcade is also of this period, and presumably also the fine stone pulpit (see page 44). There is a Norman tub font with interlaced arches. The monuments include tablets to Thomas Rogers, d1712, John Rogers, d1724 and John Ballinger, d1789.

CHELTENHAM   *St Mary*   SO 948226

The piers under the rib-vaulted crossing tower and the nave west wall are Late Norman. The unusually wide aisles with four bay arcades, the transepts and the chancel with an ornate piscina are all 14th century. The east window has a horizontal band of quatrefoils. In the chancel is a 13th century sanctus bell. The 15th century north porch has a lierne-vaulted upper chamber, opened up to the church in 1851. The south porch and north vestry are additions of 1893. The monuments include a restored early 16th century brass to William Greville and his family, an inscription by John English to his wife, d1643, and a tablet to a female of the Hughes family, d1786. There are royal arms of George III, who brought his family for a five week holiday in the town in 1788.

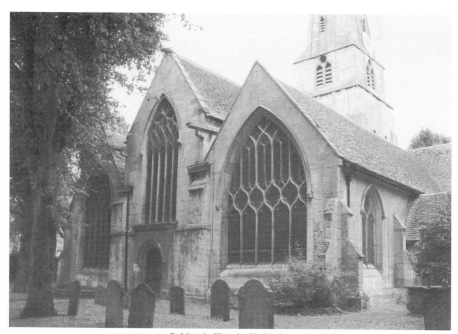

St Mary's Church, Cheltenham

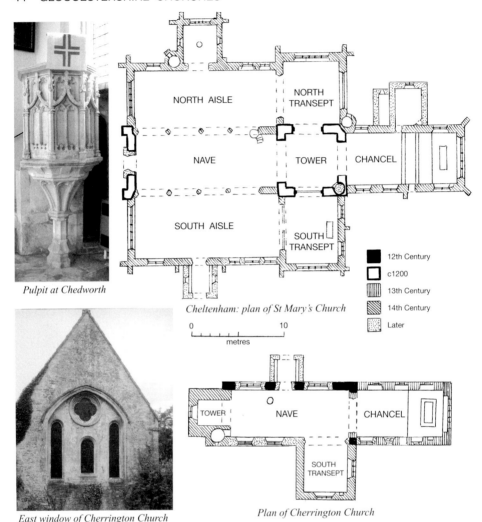

Pulpit at Chedworth

Cheltenham: plan of St Mary's Church

■	12th Century
□	c1200
▤	13th Century
▨	14th Century
▦	Later

East window of Cherrington Church

Plan of Cherrington Church

CHERRINGTON   *St Nicholas*   ST 913986

The 13th century chancel has three north lancets, a double piscina in addition to an older Norman one, and an east window with lancets flanking a round-headed central light with a quatrefoil in a circle above. The north doorway of the nave has a tympanum with two carved animals above an inscription relating to the repair of the church in 1816. The fine roof and the windows of the north wall and south transept are 15th century. The transept walls are 14th century, with an ogival-headed piscina of that date. The unbuttressed west tower is 13th century, but with a 15th century west window. There is a Norman tub font on a huge base. The altar rails are 18th century and the pulpit is made up of old parts. The monuments include inscriptions to Daniel Parker, d1650 and Joseph Trapp, d1698 and tablets to Mary Quinton, d1695, John Rodway, d1711, Thomas Coxe, d1758, and Samuel Coxe, d1786.

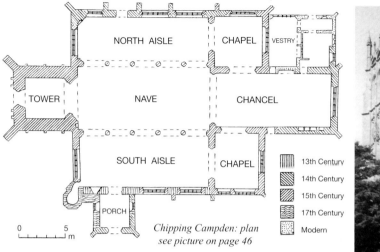

NORTH AISLE   CHAPEL   VESTRY

TOWER   NAVE   CHANCEL

SOUTH AISLE   CHAPEL

PORCH

▥	13th Century
▧	14th Century
▨	15th Century
▤	17th Century
⬚	Modern

0   5 m

Chipping Campden: plan
see picture on page 46

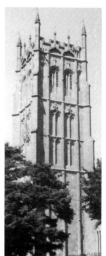

Chipping Campden

CHIPPING CAMPDEN   *St James*   SP 155395

This is a splendid late medieval church paid for by prosperous wool merchants, the town being one of the main wool-trading places in England. There are arcades of five bays of flattened four-centered arches set upon octagonal piers with concave sides, and a fine clerestory of c1500-25 with quatrefoils in the tracery and a wide window set over the chancel arch. In the chancel are triple sedilia with vaulted canopies and cresting. The west tower has string courses dividing the three stages and diagonal buttresses rising to diagonal corner pinnacles linked by an embattled parapet. Each side has three thin pilaster strips rising the full height to form ogival arches across the parapet. The tomb recess on the north side of the chancel is 13th century, and so is much of the south aisle wall, including the main doorway and a piscina, although there has been refacing outside. Of the 14th century are the south porch bearing a male head with the long hair and beard fashionable in Edward III's reign, and the south buttresses and much of the walling of the north aisle and chancel. Additions of the 17th century are the domed circular turret at the NW corner of the north aisle, and the octagonal SW turret with its ogival-shaped roof. The church was restored in the 1870s and the north vestry mostly rebuilt in 1960. Only the east window retains medieval stained glass.

On the east wall of the south aisle is part of a Norman font with 13th century decoration. In glass cases are altar hangings and two copes, all of c1400-1480. There are fine brasses of the wool merchant William Grevil, d1401, and his wife, d1386, shown under canopies, and there are smaller brasses to William Welley, d1450 and his wife Alice, William Gibbys, d1484 with his wife and children, and John Lethenard, d1487 and his wife. Under a canopy with twelve marble columns are recumbent effigies of Sir Baptist Hicks, Lord Campden, d1629 and his wife. He donated the pulpit, as recorded in an inscription on it, and the late 15th century eagle lectern. On a tomb chest are recumbent effigies of Thomas Smythe, d1593 and his wives and children. Edward Noel, Viscount Campden, 1642 and his wife Juliana are depicted in shrouds on a monument dated 1664. There are busts of Penelope Noel, d1633, and Lady Anne Noel, d1636, and tablets to William Bartholomew, d1660, and James Izod, d1795. Outside, west of the south porch is the 18th century family tomb of the Woodwards, master masons.

Chipping Campden Church

CHURCHAM   *St Andrew*   SO 769182

The church is Early Norman, although it was much restored after a fire in 1876, and neither the north doorway or the spire represent what was there before. One Norman window survives on the north side. The figure-sculpture over the north doorway is thought to be Romano-British work of the 3rd century. Red wall paintings remain on the south doorway. The 15th century font has quatrefoils. Outside the church is an earlier font bowl. There are tablets to William Harris, d1738, and Richard Green, d1786.

CHURCHDOWN   *St Bartholomew*   SO 882191

The church lies on top of a high hill and is visible for miles around. Rather curiously the three storey rib-vaulted 13th century north porch faces the slope rather than the easy approach. It contains a priest's chamber with a fireplace. and is adorned with medieval graffiti. The nave is Norman and the south aisle has a four bay Late Norman arcade. A piscina from the aisle has been moved into the chancel. The windows are mostly 15th or 16th century, except for one of the 17th century on the south side. The 14th century font has trefoil-headed niches on the pedestal and niches with crocketted canopies on the octagonal bowl. The pulpit is of 1631, and there are 17th and 18th century pews. There is a tablet to Sir Robert Austen, d1743. Figures from an Elizabethan tomb are built into the outside of the south wall.

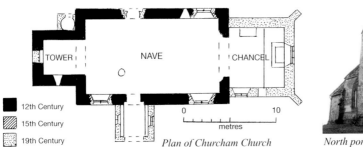

TOWER   NAVE   CHANCEL

■ 12th Century
▨ 15th Century
▧ 19th Century

0   10
metres

Plan of Churcham Church

North porch at Churchdown

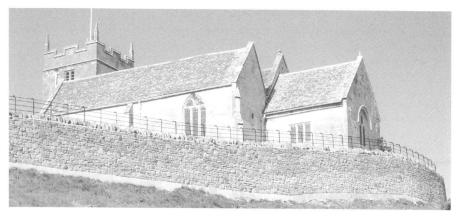

Churchdown Church

Pulpit at Cirencester   *Cirencester Church*

CIRENCESTER   *St John the Baptist*   SP 023021

Of a large Norman cruciform church dating from the same time as Henry I's founda-tion of an Augustinian abbey to the north c1120 there remains only a blocked round arch which was an altar recess on the east side of the south transept. The abbey itself replaced one of the largest Saxon minster churches in England, a 52m long fully aisled structure nine bays long with an east apse over a crypt. The piers remain of a two bay arcade built c1180 on the south side of the widened chancel. The arches are 13th century, when the chancel was given a longer new east end with triple lancets and a Lady Chapel was built against the northern aisle of the chancel, its arch from the north transept still remaining. The nave was then widened to its present width. Of the 1270s are windows with Y-tracery on each side at the east end of the chancel, and the arch from the south aisle into the south chapel, whilst c1300 the south chapel was rebuilt to form the chapel of St John the Baptist. In the 1350s the chancel arch was widened and clerestory windows added over the chancel arcades. A doorway high up suggests that there was at that time a rood screen in the form of a bridge.

The arms of Henry IV appear on the dripmould of the west doorway of the tower. This work seems to have been paid for from gifts by the king from the estates of Tho-mas Holland, Earl of Kent and the Earl of Salisbury, who were seized and executed by the townsfolk when they rebelled in 1399. Until demolition of surrounding houses c1912 the lower part of the tower, with right-angled buttresses, was mostly hidden, and rich panelling is confined to the upper parts, where there are diagonal buttresses.

In the mid 15th century the fine stone pulpit was provided and a chantry chapel was formed in the widened east part of the south aisle. The chapel retains a fine oak screen with the arms of the Garstang family of wool merchants and an original door with its closing ring. About the same time Richard Dixton, d1438 and William Prelatte, d1462 had work begun on a guild chapel of the Holy Trinity with an arcade of four bays between it and the north aisle. The chapel contains their brasses and that of chaplain Ralph Parsons, d1478 (whose cope survives in a glass case) and the Yorkist badge of the Falcon and Fetterlock appears on the apex of each arch of the arcade. The rere-dos has emblems relating to the Danvers family, although it was originally much more blatantly decorated with Yorkist emblems. Also in this period the Lady Chapel was rebuilt and given three new arches with a stone screen towards St Catharine's Chapel, which was itself given a new arcade towards the chancel. It was lengthened eastwards c1460 when a new chantry of St Catharine and St Nicholas was founded here by John Chedworth, Bishop of Lincoln. He sponsored the wall paintings of St Christopher and St Catherine on either side of the altar. In 1508 Abbot John Hakebourne provided the chapel with a fan-vault similar to that then provided in the abbey cloister. Both this chapel and the Lady Chapel retain late 15th century screens and the latter has an 18th century marble font. In the Garstang Chapel are early 18th century busts of Rebecca Powell and her husbands William Georges and Thomas Powell.

A porch flanked by octagonal turrets was added in the 1490s. A much larger struc-ture with panelling and fan-vaulting was added soon after. Two upper storeys were used for financial transactions. It became the town hall and the upper parts were rebuilt in 1831 using the old materials but without the uppermost floor, so as to make one single large and lofty upper chamber. Between 1516 and 1530 new nave arcades and a clerestory above were built. Shields on the piers bear the arms or merchants' marks of the many contributors, and Henry VIII's royal arms appear over the window over the chancel arch, under which a new screen and rood loft were set up in the 1530s.

The Lady Chapel at Cirencester

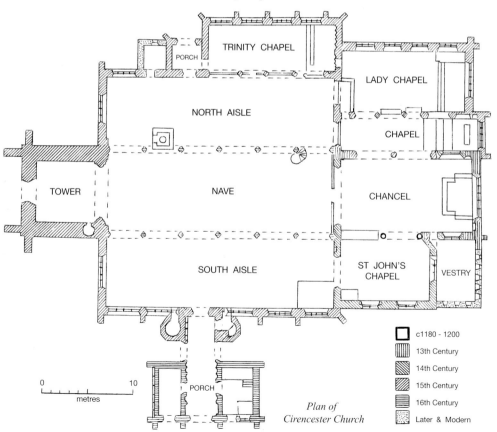

TRINITY CHAPEL

PORCH

LADY CHAPEL

NORTH AISLE

CHAPEL

TOWER

NAVE

CHANCEL

SOUTH AISLE

ST JOHN'S CHAPEL

VESTRY

0 ... 10

metres

PORCH

Plan of Cirencester Church

- c1180 - 1200
- 13th Century
- 14th Century
- 15th Century
- 16th Century
- Later & Modern

By the 1540s all of the windows at Cirencester contained stained glass. Despite some windows being broken in 1642 during attempts to send in food to prisoners held here by Prince Rupert, and subsequent neglect, much of the glass survived until the 18th century. In the 1790s what remained was mostly reset in the east and west windows under the supervision of Samuel Lysons. The glass was rearranged again in 1939 and 1946 and some parts were returned to the windows that they had come from. There is also much 19th century glass. The church has a very fine set of plate, and on show is a cup dated 1535 with the badge of the family of Anne Boleyn. There are two fine chandeliers of 1701. The Lady Chapel contains brasses of John Gunter, d1626 and his wife and fragments of several others. In the NE corner is a tomb with recumbent effigies of Humfry Bridges, d1598, and his wife, d1620. There is a semi-reclining effigy of Sir Thomas Master, d1680. Other monuments are to William Master, d1661, John Cripps, 1793 and Johnathan Skin, d1791. The effigy of a merchant in St Catherine's Chapel is thought to be Richard Osmund, d1517. Marble kneeling figures of George Monox, d1638 and his wife lie in St John the Baptist's Chapel. There are many tablets in the nave and in the north aisle are a brass to the wool-merchant Philip Warner, d1587, and a coffin lid with a foliated cross of William de Cheltenham, d1306. Apart from monuments already mentioned the Trinity Chapel has brasses of wool-merchants Reginald Spycer, d1442 and Robert Page, d1434 and their wives, and busts of the first and second Earls Bathurst, d1776 and 1794.

Brass at Cirencester

Clapton-on-the-Hill Church

CLAPTON-ON-THE-HILL   *St James*   SP 763180

This small church was a chapel-of-ease to Bourton-on-the-Water. The south doorway with a lintel and small tympanum and the jambs of the chancel arch are late 12th century. The chancel arch itself is 13th century, the likely date of the inscription on the abacus on the north side promising an indulgence of a thousand days in return for saying a Pater and an Ave penitently and devoutly. Also 13th century are the south porch and two lancet windows. Several square-headed windows and the damaged mural texts date from a restoration of 1670. A tub-shaped Norman font has later been modified to fit onto an octagonal shaft. The best of several ledger stones is that of John Woodman dated 1693. In the churchyard is the base of a cross. See plan on page 53.

COALEY   *St Bartholomew*   SO 771018

The church was entirely rebuilt in 1854-8, except for the diagonally buttressed late 14th or early 15th century tower. There is a brass to Daniel Stayno, d1630.

COATES   *St Matthew*   SO 972010

The Norman south doorway has a chevron-moulded arch, a billeted hood-mould and shafts with scalloped capitals. During the restoration of 1861 the plain Norman chancel arch was reset into the chancel north wall. The south arcade of c1190 has three bays of pointed arches on circular piers with moulded capitals. The aisle itself seems to be 13th century, with one lancet east of the porch, and three in the east wall, plus a trefoil-headed piscina. The priest's doorway is also 13th century, and there are several 15th century south windows. A chantry chapel with a tomb-recess, piscina and one 14th century window is most unusually set against the western half of the north wall. Also 14th century are the east window and the ashlar-faced west tower with a quadripartite vault and diagonal buttresses supporting pilaster quoins with crocketed pinnacles. In the west side is a Latin inscription requesting prayers for Rector John Wiat, who paid for the work, and the date 1733 referring to repairs. The font bowl is Norman, but set on a later stem and base. Some 15th century woodwork remains in the screen. There are 17th and 18th century brass inscriptions.

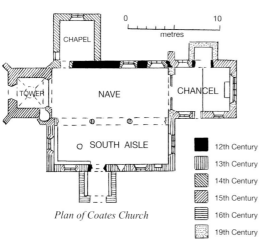

Plan of Coates Church

0 — 10 metres

CHAPEL

TOWER   NAVE   CHANCEL

SOUTH AISLE

■ 12th Century
▨ 13th Century
▨ 14th Century
▨ 15th Century
▤ 16th Century
▨ 19th Century

Coaley Church

Effigy at Coberley   *Low-side window at Coberley*

COBERLEY *St Giles* SO 966147

The Norman nave and chancel were rebuilt in 1869-72 , leaving only a fragment of chevron ornamentation on the north side. Sir Thomas Berkeley's south chapel of c1340 was also refaced, although it retains original features such as the ballflower-edged quatrefoil low-side window and two other windows with flowing tracery and fine head-stops. In the chapel are effigies of Sir Thomas, and his wife, who was the mother of Dick Whittington by a subsequent marriage, plus a young girl carrying a glove, and also man in civilian dress under a cinquefoiled tomb recess. There is also an indent of a 16th century brass and a 17th century tablet to the Castleman family. The diagonally buttressed west tower is late 14th or early 15th century. The pulpit is Jacobean and there is a late 17th century altar table. There is a stump of a medieval cross in the churchyard, which is reached from the road through a gate into the yard of a house.

COLD ASTON *St Andrew* SP 128199

The chancel has one small blocked Norman north window and the nave has a blocked Norman north doorway with a worn tympanum and a fine south doorway with shafts and an arch of three orders with a roll-moulding, a double billet and diapering. The honeycombed tympanum has an arch with rosettes and there are leaves and tendrils on the lintel. The eastern third of the nave has thinner walls from a later rebuilding and the chancel arch dates from the restoration of 1875. In the porch are reset Norman stones and part of a 14th century piscina. The 15th century west tower has diagonal buttressing lower down but straight angle buttresses with pinnacles higher up. Inside it has a tierceron vault. The chancel has no east window and instead there are remains of an elaborate 14th century reredos. Nearby in the north wall is an Easter Sepulchre, whilst on the south is a 13th century pillar-piscina and a credence-shelf in the splay of a window. There is a coloured Baroque stone monument to Giles Carter, d1664, signed by Reeve of Gloucester.

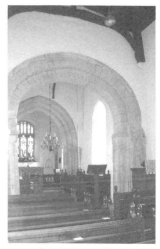

Coln St Dennis Church

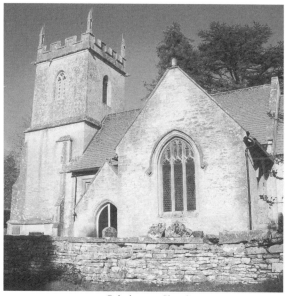

Colesbourne Church

COLESBOURNE *St James* SO 004134

The chancel arch is late 13th century but set on Norman jambs, and the lower part of a Norman doorway survives in the nave north wall. The chancel south wall is 14th century but the east and north walls were rebuilt together with the north transept in the restoration of 1851-2, when a north chapel was removed along with the nave clerestory. The south transept with a trefoiled piscina, squint and old roof is 14th century. The north transept also retains a squint. Of the 15th century are the diagonally buttressed west tower, the font and the fine stone pulpit. There are minor fragments of late medieval glass. The embossed tile with a crucifix on the outside of the east wall is probably 14th century.

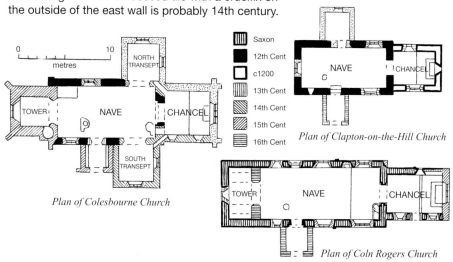

▥	Saxon
■	12th Cent
□	c1200
▥	13th Cent
▧	14th Cent
▨	15th Cent
▤	16th Cent

0 — 10 metres

NORTH TRANSEPT

TOWER NAVE CHANCEL

SOUTH TRANSEPT

Plan of Colesbourne Church

NAVE CHANCEL

Plan of Clapton-on-the-Hill Church

TOWER NAVE CHANCEL

Plan of Coln Rogers Church

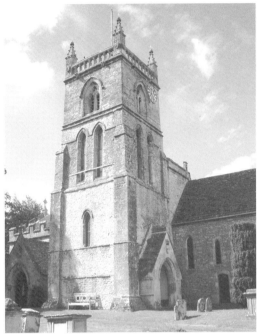

Coln St Aldwyns Church   *Saxon long-and-short work at Coln Rogers*

COLN ROGERS   *St Andrew*   SP 088098

The nave and chancel are Saxon work with a round arch between them, long-and-short quoins on three of the nave corners, four pilaster strips (one with a Saxon sundial), and one tiny window in the chancel north wall. The blocked north doorway has a cinquefoiled arch externally, but the inner part seems original Saxon work. The tub font and the south doorway with a plain tympanum and shafts with scalloped capitals are early 12th century. The chancel was later lengthened and given two south lancets and a priest's doorway, but the east wall is 15th century. Probably of the middle of the 16th century are the south porch and the small tower inserted within the west end of the nave. There is a medieval oak chest with original ironwork and one north window contains a 15th century stained glass figure of St Margaret. There is a tablet to Jeremiah Millington, d1796. See the plan on page 53 and picture on page 4.

COLN ST ALDWYNS   *St John the Baptist*   SP 144052

The late 12th century south doorway has three orders and lozenge and chevron mouldings on keeled jamb shafts, and dragonheads to the hoodmould. It contains an old door with an iron latch. Over a blocked Norman window west of the porch is a figure of a demon chasing a man whose hand is held in his jaws. The south transeptal tower with clasping buttresses is of c1200-25, although the upper stage may be of the 1280s, and the pierced parapet with pinnacles, gargoyles and the royal arms and the arms of the de Clares and Gloucester Abbey is 15th century. There are lancets in the 13th century chancel, and the nave has 14th century windows and a chandelier of c1767. The north transept and the chancel arch are 19th century.

COLN ST DENNIS   *St James*   SP 086110

The nave, the central tower, and the chancel with pilaster buttresses, an original piscina and shafts for an intended vault, are all Norman. There are billeted hoodmoulds on the north and south doorways, the latter having shafts with scalloped capitals. Of the 15th century are the top part of the tower, the eastern arch (on older piers) under it, the east and north windows of the chancel, and the nave parapet and roof, plus one window and the north porch. The north door is dated 1637. There are tablets to John Bridges, d1679, John Kirrill, d1762, and Sir Benjamin Kemp, d1777. See pp 6 & 53.

COMPTON ABDALE   *St Oswald*   SP 059166

The 15th century west tower was built at the expense of St Oswald's Priory at Gloucester. It has a stair-turret, diagonal buttresses with animals on the off-sets, and fragment of old glass in the west window. Corbel heads suggest a date c1420 for the north doorway. Also 15th century are the east window with a small embattled transom, one large south window, and the four bay arcade, but the church was much restored in 1881 and 1904-5. On the south wall is a very worn figure of St George and the Dragon.

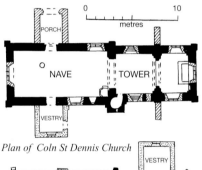

Plan of Coln St Dennis Church

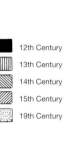

Plan of Condicote Church

CONDICOTE   *St Nicholas*   SP 152283

The nave has an original Norman west wall with stringcourses and a south doorway of two orders with chevrons, cable and bead mouldings and shafts. The tympanum and lintel are diapered with stars. Fragments of the north doorway are reset in the south porch built in 1888, when two neo-Norman windows were inserted into a genuine Norman chancel with a 13th century piscina. The nave north wall has one 14th century window with flowing tracery, and the south wall has a three-light 15th century window fitted with an image bracket. During the 15th century the Norman font was recut into an octagonal shape.

■ 12th Century
▥ 13th Century
▧ 14th Century
▨ 15th Century
▦ 19th Century

Compton Abdale Church   *Condicote Church*

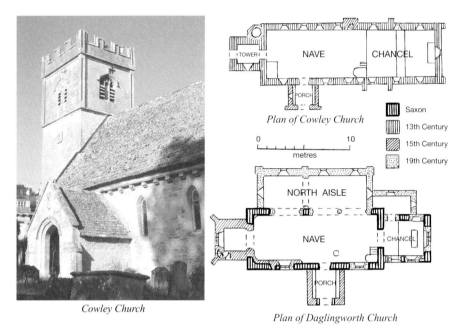

Plan of Cowley Church

NAVE   CHANCEL

TOWER

PORCH

Saxon

13th Century

15th Century

19th Century

0   10
metres

Cowley Church

Plan of Daglingworth Church

NORTH AISLE

NAVE   CHANCEL

PORCH

CORSE   *St Margaret*   SO 789265

The nave, chancel, and west tower and spire are all 14th century, with several windows of that date. Other windows are 16th century, the period of the timber-framed north porch. The nave has a ceiled wagon roof with moulded tiebeams and wall-plates. The Norman font has scallops and a band at the bottom with cable and pellet moulding. There is a painted tablet to John Clark, d1787.

COWLEY   *St Mary*   SP 966147

The early 13th century nave has a roll-moulded south doorway and lancet windows. The tiny tower has a fancy 15th century top with panelled angle-pilasters set on a plain 13th century base. It has a sundial on the south side. The ashlar-faced chancel is mid 13th century and has a trefoil-headed piscina and a row on lancets on each side and one facing east. An early 14th century effigy of a priest lies in a recess in the north wall. The nave has a 14th century wagon roof and there is a 15th century porch. The Norman font has chevrons and a band of lozenges and triangles. There is a 15th century pulpit. The church lies in the grounds of the adjacent manor house.

CRANHAM   *St James*   SO 891124

The 15th century west tower has diagonal buttresses, carvings of sheep-shears and a parapet with gargoyles. The south aisle with a three bay arcade is also 15th century but has a west lancet of the 13th century, perhaps reset. The chancel was mostly rebuilt in 1894-5, when the north aisle and porch were added, but a scene of the Crucifixion remains on the east wall. The screen of c1500 has open panels with cusped heads and quatrefoils and a roodbeam with a vine motif. There are monuments to Obadiah Done, d1738, Elizabeth Sadler, d1744, Richard Done, d1740, and William Hunter, d1792, amongst others. There are several notable tombs in the churchyard.

CUTSDEAN *St James* SP 088301

There is a 17th century font in the church, which was rebuilt in 1863 except for the 14th century west tower.

DAGLINGWORTH *Holy Rood* SO 994050

Of a Saxon nave there remain the south wall with long-and-short work at the corners, a blocked south window with the head cut from a single stone and the south doorway surmounted by an original Saxon sundial. A second window was taken off to Barnsley church. The chancel arch imposts and the nave NE corner also survived the rebuilding of 1845-50, from which period date most of the chancel, the vestry, and the north aisle and its arcade. The 15th century south porch incorporates Saxon work from a west doorway removed when the tower was added and the crucifix high up on the east wall is also thought to be Saxon. Of c1050 are the sculptures showing St St Peter with a key, Our Lord enthroned, and a Christ on the Cross flanked by Longinus and Stephaton, respectively carrying a spear and scourge and a reed and a sponge. In the vestry is a Roman panel with an inscription to the Mothergoddess, in which two narrow lancet lights have been cut. There is a Norman stone altar which has come from an upper priest's chamber built inside the nave west end. There is a 15th century font. The west window has some old glass. There are 18th century altar rails. The monuments include tablets to John Haines, d1771, Edmund Hinton, d1773. In the churchyard are the base and shaft of a 14th century cross and several late 17th century table-tombs.

Two of the 11th century sculptures at Daglingworth

DAYLESFORD *St Peter* SP 243260

The Norman church replacing a Saxon minster was rebuilt c1820 and replaced in the 1860s by the present cruciform building. The only original parts are an arch in the vestry and the south doorway. There is a brass dated 1632 depicting William Gardiner.

Interior of Odda's Chapel at Deerhurst

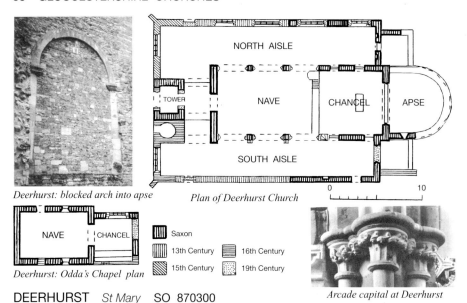

Deerhurst: blocked arch into apse

Plan of Deerhurst Church

Deerhurst: Odda's Chapel plan

Saxon

13th Century   16th Century

15th Century   19th Century

Arcade capital at Deerhurst

DEERHURST   *St Mary*   SO 870300

Much of this church existed by 804, when it was serving a Benedictine priory. It then comprised a tall nave with pairs of porticus or side-chapels added to each side, and a west porch. Alterations of the 10th century (with herringbone masonry here and there) are the polygonal apse with corner pilasters, now in ruins, the addition of further porticus, and the upper parts of the tower built over the porch. This part has a double triangular-headed window with fluted and reeded pilasters looking east into the nave. Below is a doorway which must have served a wooden gallery. There are beast-stops on the hoodmould of the blocked chancel arch and on a doorway in the porch and on a doorway to the former cloister. Doorways on two levels show that the eastern porticus, at least, were of two storeys. Further west the porticus now form aisles with fine three bay arcades inserted in the early 13th century. Further arches link the aisles with the west porch. There is a carved angel on the apse and a carving of the Virgin and Child on the west porch. The late 9th century font has narrow bands of vine-scroll above and below a broad band of double trumpet-spiral ornament. For many years it was in use as a washing tub at a farm and only restored to the church c1860. The windows of the aisles and clerestorey are 14th and 16th century. The south aisle west window contains glass of c1310 and c1450. This aisle contains medieval pews. The altar rails are of c1600. There are fine brasses of Sir John Cassey, c1400 in a judge's robes, with his wife, with her pet dog Terri at her feet. Two other brasses depict early 16th century females, and there is a 14th century coffin lid with a foliated cross upon it.

About 200 yards south of the church is an unusually complete Late Saxon chapel consisting of nave and chancel. It formed part of the adjoining house until 1965, the nave having contained a tall kitchen. In it are two double-splayed original windows, one still retaining part of a wooden window-frame. The north doorway and the chancel arch of through stones with a square-sectioned hoodmould are horseshoe shaped. The nave has long-and-short quoins. A stone now in the Ashmolean museum records the dedication of this chapel to the Holy Trinity on 12th April 1056 by Earl Odda of Mercia in honour of his brother Aelfric, so this is a rare example of a dated Saxon church.

Exterior of Deerhurst Church

Saxon font at Deerhurst

*A picture of Odda's Chapel at
Deerhurst appears on page 57.*

Saxon arch at Deerhurst

Interior of Deerhurst Church, looking west

Didbrook Church

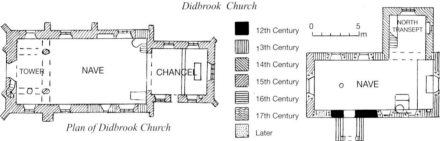

■	12th Century
▥	13th Century
▨	14th Century
▧	15th Century
▤	16th Century
▦	17th Century
▒	Later

0 ——— 5 m

Plan of Didbrook Church

Plan of Didmarton Church

DIDBROOK   *St George*   SP 055314

Only the 14th century font and parts of the 13th century nave walls pre-date the re-building of the church in the 1470s by William Whitchurch, Abbot of Hailes. The ash-lar-faced tower stands within the nave upon three arches. The chancel has a piscina, a priest's doorway and a doorway to the rood staircase. The east window has some original stained glass. The benches and lectern are old, and of the 17th century are the altar rails and the pulpit with a tester. There is a foliated cross on a 14th century cof-fin lid of a priest. Another outside in the churchyard has a human head in a crocketed canopy on the the the cross. There is also a tablet to Judge Robert Tracy, d1735.

DIDMARTON   *St Lawrence*   ST 820873

The church has a small 12th and 13th century main body and a north transept with an end window of c1300. The 15th century west end is of ashlar. A three-decker pulpit and other Georgian furnishings have survived because services were transferred to a new church of 1872 not far to the east (now in use as a house). The monuments in-clude tablets of Elizabeth Tyrrell, d1745, and Cornelius Robins, d1775. The font has a 14th century bowl, an 18th century cover, and a 12th century pedestal.

Head at Deerhurst

Didmarton Church

Norman tympanum at Dowdeswell

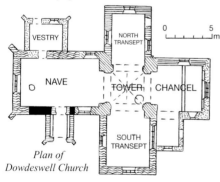

Plan of
Dowdeswell Church

Dowdeswell Church

DOWDESWELL *St Michael* SP 001199

The church is cruciform and has a late 14th century crossing arches and a tierceron vault. An inscription on the sill of the north transept west window refers to the broach-spire being rebuilt in 1577. Reset on the gable of the organ chamber of c1840 is a Norman tympanum of the Tree of Life discovered in the 19th century. The south transept of 1633 has a window with panelling rather than tracery. The nave west end is also of that period. It contains a private pew with an external entrance and steps, and there is another in the north transept. The south porch is 16th century. One nave window is 14th century. There are quatrefoils on the 15th century font. There are hatchments with the arms of Lionel Rich, and two members of the Rogers family. The oldest monuments are of Edward Rich, d1680, Baily Rich, d1723, and Richard Rogers, d1757.

North arcade at Down Ampney

Down Ampney Church

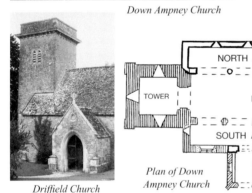

Driffield Church

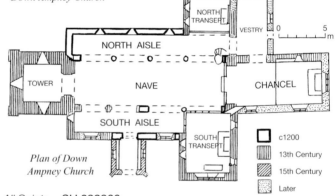

Plan of Down Ampney Church

Plan labels: NORTH TRANSEPT, VESTRY, NORTH AISLE, TOWER, NAVE, CHANCEL, SOUTH AISLE, SOUTH TRANSEPT

Scale: 0 — 5 m

Legend:
- c1200
- 13th Century
- 15th Century
- Later

DOWN AMPNEY *All Saints* SU 099966

The west tower with blind arcading at the top and flat buttresses may date from about the time of the consecration recorded in 1265, but the spire is later. There are narrow aisles and transepts, but the north transept, chancel and clerestory are mostly 19th century work. The four bay north arcade is of c1185-1200, and the south arcade is slightly later. Both have pointed arches painted in the 13th century with cinquefoil red flowers with white centres. The south transept has a squint and a trefoil-headed piscina and a credence shelf. The hexagonal font is 17th century. The chancel has a coffin lid with a foliated cross under a 13th century recess in the north wall. In the south transept are recumbent effigies of Sir Nicholas de Valers, c1300, and Margaret de Valers, c1320. In the north transept is a monument of 1637 with kneeling effigies of Sir John Hungerford and Sir Anthony Hungerford. There are tablets to Cesar Chandeler, d1754 and his wife, d1752. The fine furnishings are all late 19th century.

Down Hatherley Church

Dumbleton Church

DOWN HATHERLEY *St Mary* SO 868225

Only a diagonally buttressed 15th century west tower with gargoyles and a 16th century lead font with roses, stars and lozenges survived the rebuilding of 1860.

DRIFFIELD *St Mary* SU 074098

The tower and the pulpit and box pews and various other furnishings date from the rebuilding of 1734 and much else (especially stained glass) dates from a restoration in 1863. The south porch has an east niche which is late medieval and part of a Norman tympanum remains over the south doorway. There are several tablets to the Hanger family, Lords Coleraine.

DUMBLETON *St Peter* SP 017358

Parts remain of a corbel table with grotesque figures on the Norman nave. The north doorway has a carved tympanum and an outer arch with chevrons, although the inner arch is 16th century, as is that of the 13th century south doorway, now within a porch of 1905. The late 13th century west tower has a 15th century embattled top. The nave also has one 13th century lancet window. The north transept has 14th century windows. The chancel was mostly rebuilt in 1862, and there is a modern organ chamber. The octagonal font is dated 1661. There are kneeling effigies of Sir Charles Percy, d1628 and his wife with one infant. Other monuments of the Cocks family include a bust of Charles, d1654, Sir Richard, d1684, Frances, d1723, Sir Robert, d1765, Elizabeth, d1749, and Dorothy, d1767. Two Jacobean table-tombs lie in the churchyard.

DUNTISBOURNE ABBOTS   *St Peter*   SO 970079

The Late Norman west tower has one original south window, a late 13th century window facing west, and a 15th century saddleback top with bell-openings with multiple quatrefoils. The north aisle has one window of c1300 but the two bay arcade with pointed arches and a circular pier is Late Norman. The south aisle is an addition of the 1870s, against which the original 13th century south porch has been re-erected. The chancel was late 13th century but has been mostly rebuilt and given a new triple arched chancel arch. The Norman font has tri-lobed foliage. There is medieval ironwork on the south door. There is a monument to Ann Price, d1793.

Dursley Church

DUNTISBOURNE ROUSE   *St Michael*   SO 985061

The Saxon nave has long-and-short work at the corners, a blocked north doorway with a flat lintel on massive imposts, and a triangular-headed south doorway. The chancel is Early Norman and is built over a vaulted crypt chapel because of the sloping site. Both levels have original windows. The nave has an old roof with braced collars and moulded tie-beams and two lancet windows, one of them trefoil headed. One window is 15th century, as is the tiny west tower, although the saddle-backed top is dated 1587. The south porch has a sundial dated 1756. There is trilobed foliage on five of the eight sides of the 13th century font. The wall painting and the stalls with miserichords of grotesque heads in the chancel are late medieval. The pulpit is Jacobean and there are 17th and 18th century pews and panelling. Outside is a 14th century cross.

Duntisbourne Rouse Church

DURSLEY *St James* ST 758981

The wide north aisle has a 14th century east window, and the font is also of that date. The east end of the south aisle was a chapel and retains an arcade of two 13th century arches. Otherwise the arcades are mid 15th century, the date of the south wall and the lierne-vaulted south porch with an upper chamber. The west tower was built in 1707-9, still in the Gothic style with diagonal buttresses. It replaced a tower and spire that collapsed in 1699. A choir vestry and organ chamber were added on the south side when the chancel was rebuilt in 1867. In the south aisle is a 15th century cadaver effigy, probably of one of the Tanner family of merchants.

DYMOCK *St Mary* SO 701312

The large, unusual blank arcading of the south side of the chancel belonged to an impressive Early Norman church of c1100 which also had an apse and a central tower, both now gone. The chancel arch and the south doorway with figured volute capitals and a Tree of Life tympanum are additions of c1140. The apse was replaced by a square end in the 14th century, and also of that period are the north transept and south chapel and the western doorway and corner buttresses. A diagonally-buttressed west tower with a short spire was added in the mid 15th century. The oldest of the two fonts is a wooden one of the 1660s. There are fragments of old glass in the porch. The oldest monument is that of William Hankins, d1771.

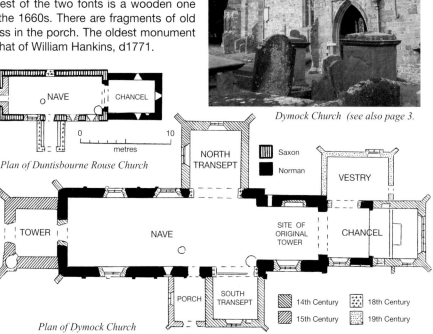

Dymock Church (see also page 3.

Plan of Duntisbourne Rouse Church

Plan of Dymock Church

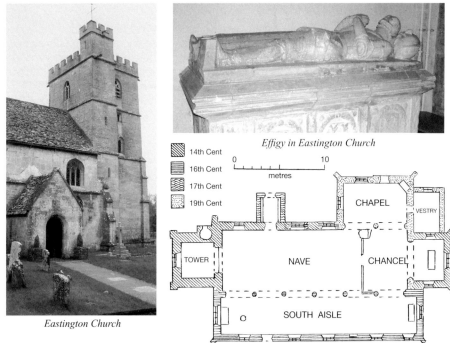

Effigy in Eastington Church

14th Cent
16th Cent
17th Cent
19th Cent

0   10
metres

CHAPEL
VESTRY

TOWER   NAVE   CHANCEL

SOUTH AISLE

Eastington Church

Plan of Eastington Church

EASTINGTON St Michael SO 782058

The 14th century west tower has a square stair-turret on the NE corner. The chancel was also of that period. The rest is mostly late medieval, with straight headed windows in the south aisle, where the doorway has the initials of the Duke of Buckingham, executed by Henry VIII in 1521. His initials also appear on glass reset in the organ chamber. The east window has fine tracery and a dripmould ending in angels with shields. The arcade inside is of six bays with octagonal piers. There is a Norman tub font. One north window has some medieval glass. Monuments of the Stephens family include recumbent effigies of Edward, d1587, and his wife, brass inscriptions to Margaret, d1591, Catherine, d1632, Anne, d1722, Catherine, d1725, and Richard, d1705, and others to Edward, d1587, Richard, d1660, Robert, d1675, Nathaniel, 1792, and Henry, d1794. There is a brass depicting Elizabeth Knevet, d1518, in an heraldic mantle. Other monuments include those of Henry Willis, d1794, and John James, d1790.

EASTLEACH MARTIN St Michael & St Martin SP 203052

The responds of the chancel arch and the south and north doorways (the latter blocked) are Early Norman. The chancel is mostly late 13th century, with triple east lancets and some of the side lancets trefoil-headed. There is also a trefoil-headed niche in the east wall of the south porch of the same period. Near it is a window with intersecting tracery. The 14th century north transept has good windows of that period. The tower has a crossloop for the staircase, a hipped roof, and a late 14th century west window with some old glass. Several other windows have fragments of old glass. The font and some of the benches are 15th century. Other pews and the pulpit are 17th century. The chest is dated 1662. The shaft and steps remain of a 14th century churchyard cross.

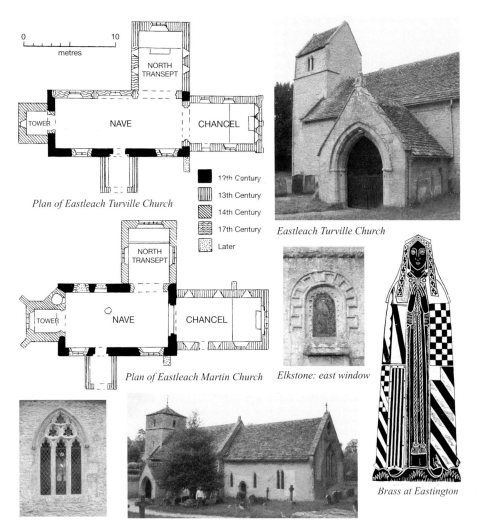

0 ⌞⌞⌞⌞⌞⌞⌞⌞⌞⌞⌞ 10
metres

NORTH TRANSEPT

TOWER | NAVE | CHANCEL

Plan of Eastleach Turville Church

■ 12th Century
▦ 13th Century
▨ 14th Century
▧ 17th Century
▦ Later

NORTH TRANSEPT

TOWER | NAVE | CHANCEL

Plan of Eastleach Martin Church

Eastleach Turville Church

Elkstone: east window

Brass at Eastington

Eastleach Martin: window   Eastleach Martin Church

EASTLEACH TURVILLE *St Andrew* SP 203055

The Norman south doorway has shafts with scalloped capitals and a tympanum show-ing Christ in Majesty in a vesica supported by angels. All that remains of a small chantry chapel of c1200 is a blocked arch in the chancel north wall. Of the 13th century are the south porch with an image niche in the east wall, the chancel arch and most of the chancel with triple east lancets with moulded internal arches, the north transept with lancet windows, and the arches which remain of the former north aisle. Under these arches are 17th century windows. From the 14th century are the saddleback roofed tower, the window between it and the porch, and the tomb canopy with ballflowers and a foliated cross-slab hidden behind the organ in the transept. Old woodwork includes the reading desk of 1632, the chest of 1678 and the altar table and lectern.

Effigy in Ebrington Church

EBRINGTON   *St Eadburga*   SP 184400

The Norman doorway has three orders of chevrons and diaperwork on the tympanum. In the 13th century a porch was added in front, with a quatrefoil east opening towards a south aisle with an arcade of two bays and a squint towards the large and heavily restored 13th century chancel. Over the priest's doorway is a 17th century sundial and the arms of the Keyts family. The 15th century west tower has diagonal buttresses and heads under the abaci of the tower arch. A few bench ends and the font with quatre-foils are also 15th century. The pulpit and lectern are 17th century and there are royal arms of 1725. The aisle east window has 17th century heraldic glass. There is a painted recumbent effigy of Lord Chief Justice Sir John Fortescue, d1484. There are also busts of Sir Keyt, d1662, and his wife, and a monument to Sir William Keyt, d1632.

EDGEWORTH   *St Mary*   SO 948060

The nave is partly Saxon, with a mutilated north doorway of that period. The Normans lengthened the nave eastwards and provided a south doorway with chevrons and a new chancel with a corbel-table and pilaster buttresses. The original east window survives, although a triple of lancets was provided in the 13th century. Other lancets in the side walls (one with old stained glass) and the south porch were much restored in the 1860s. There are 14th and 16th century windows in the nave and a 15th century west tower with gargoyles. The font with quatrefoils and some of the bench ends are 15th century. Outside is a churchyard cross.

Norman corbel table at Edgeworth

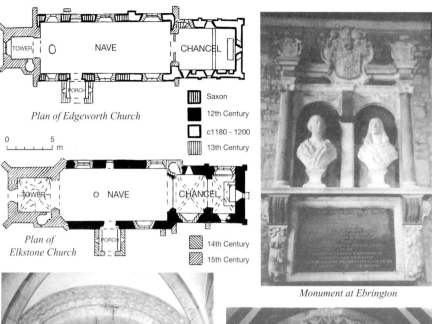

Plan of Edgeworth Church

0 ____ 5
⌞_____⌟ m

	Saxon
	12th Century
	c1180 - 1200
	13th Century

Plan of
Elkstone Church

| | 14th Century |
| | 15th Century |

Monument at Ebrington

Vaulted sanctuary at Elkstone

Norman tympanum at Elkstone

ELKSTONE St John SO 907123

Much of the church dates from the 1160s, when it had a tower between the nave and the chancel, although the narrow north doorway may be older. The south doorway has a tympanum depicting Christ in Majesty, with emblems of the Evangelists and the hand of God the Father. It is set on a shouldered arch with capitals with grotesque heads. There are corbel-tables on both sides and the east window has an outer band of crenellations and an inner border of pellets. Internally it has chevrons and a rebate for a shutter. The space under the original tower has a 14th century quadripartite rib-vault and a NW staircase now just leading to a dovecote over the vault. The rebuilt west arch has chevrons, a hoodmould with pellets and dragon headstops. The sanctuary is reached through an arch with chevrons and has an original vault with rolls on either side of a square band and a central boss with four grotesque masks. The late 14th century west tower has a tierceron vault, diagonal buttresses supporting pilasters and three stages marked by string-courses. There are gargoyles and sculptures of musicians and the west window has winged angel stops bearing shields. The nave roof and the octagonal font with quatrefoils are 15th century. A pulpit of 1609 is set on an older stone base. Outside, near the porch, are two good mid-17th century table tombs.

Elmstone Hardwicke Church

ELMORE *St John the Baptist*   SO 767150

A 13th century five bay arcade with rectangular piers divides a nave and north aisle of equal width. There is a single wide arch between the chancel and the north chapel, now a vestry, in which is an east window with intersecting tracery. The lower parts of the tower west of the aisle are 13th century, the top being late 14th or 15th century. The priest's doorway with an ogival head and the adjacent window are 14th century. There are 15th century windows along the south side and north and south timber-framed porches. One five-light window on the south side is early 16th century. On a tomb chest of 1472 is an incised slab depicting Johannes Gyse. There are other monuments to William Guise, d1642, William Guise d1716, William James, d1744, & Daniel Ellis, d1797.

ELMSTONE HARDWICKE *St Mary Magdalene* SO 920260

The chancel has 14th century windows, and there is a fine late 14th century west tower with an image in a niche, gargoyles, and musicians forming the stops of the belfry windows. In the 1871 the south aisle was refaced and given three new arches for its arcade, and the south porch has also been rebuilt. The west two bays of the arcade, however, are Norman and the piscinae in the aisle and chancel are 13th century.

EVENLODE *St Edward* SO 220290

The oldest features are the Late Norman chancel arch and one northern lancet window. The 14th century south aisle has an arcade of two bays with an elongated octagonal pier, sedilia, and a piscina in the sill of one of the two south windows. The vestry was added during a restoration in 1879. The font and the pulpit of oak are 15th century. See plan on page 72 and picture on page 9.

FAIRFORD *St Mary* SP 151012

Apart from the 14th century crossing piers the church was entirely rebuilt at the expense of the wool merchant John Tame, d1500, and his son Sir Edmund, d1534, to whom there are tomb chests bearing fine brasses depicting them with their wives. On the tower buttresses are hatted figures with swords. The symbols and arms of the Despencers, the earls of Warwick and the Yorkists may be older wortk reset but Tame's own merchant's mark appears with them on the parapet and his arms appear on the west side, where there is a figure of Christ. There is also fine sculpture on the stringcourses below the parapets of the rest of the church. The panelled south porch has a fan-vault and an original inner door with a smaller door set within it. The arcades have piers of a complex section with sixteen shafts and four-centred arches. There are triple sedilia with embattled canopies and an original door opposite to the vestry. Because of this vestry the east window of the adjoining Lady Chapel is set very high up. The roofs are original and have angel corbels, and those in the south chapel include Tame's arms and symbols of the Passion.

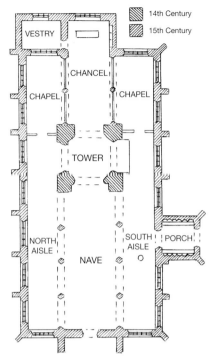

14th Century
15th Century

VESTRY

CHANCEL

CHAPEL   CHAPEL

TOWER

NORTH
AISLE   SOUTH   PORCH
AISLE
NAVE

Plan of Fairford Church

Fairford Church

Furnishings include a 15th century font with the badge of Edward IV, stalls with miserichords carved with grotesque figures, a fine set of early 16th century screens with the emblems of Katherine of Aragon, an altar table of 1626 and a lectern with original 12th century feet and a bible of 1551. Other monuments include recumbent effigies of 1560 of the widow of Sir Edmund Tame II and her second husband Roger Lygon, plus a tablet to Muriel Oldisworth, d1754.

Fine though they are, the architecture, furnishings and monuments of the church at Fairford are overshadowed by a nearly complete set of original stained glass filling the huge windows, mostly of four lights, but with five at the aisle ends. It is thought to have come from the workshop of Bernard Flower, who also provided glass for Henry VII's magnificent Lady Chapel at Westminster Abbey. The glass was repaired and cleaned after removal during World War II and the scheme in the upper part of the seven light west window wrecked by a gale in 1703 is a 19th century reproduction. In the NE part of the north aisle are Old Testiment scenes such as the Incarnation, Adam and Eve, Gideon's Fleece and the Burning Bush. Windows in the Lady Chapel have the story of the Virgin Mary, the Annunciation and events in Christ's childhood, whilst the chapel east window has the Assumption. The chancel east window has the Passion over the events of Holy Week and the south window here has the Deposition, the Burial and the Harrowing of Hell. The Transfiguration appears in the central light of the east window of the Corpus Christi Chapel, and other windows continue the story of the Gospels up to Pentecost. The twelve apostles appear in the nave, then the evangelists, whilst the west window has a Last Judgement. The north clerestory windows show traitors and persecutors of the Christian Church, with demons in the tracery lights.

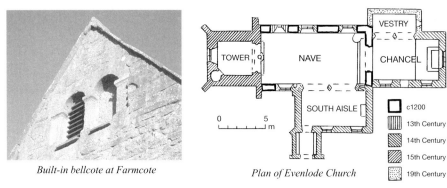

Built-in bellcote at Farmcote

Plan of Evenlode Church

c1200
13th Century
14th Century
15th Century
19th Century

VESTRY

TOWER   NAVE   CHANCEL

SOUTH AISLE

0   5
m

FARMCOTE   *St Faith*   SP 061291

Only the Norman nave now survives. Original are the north doorway, the round chancel arch with a roll-moulding, and a double bellcote now partly built into the heightened west gable. The window below it is late 14th century. The south side has a doorway with decorated spandrels and windows of the early 16th century and there are benches of that period. The piscina has a wooden pillar. Four moulded shafts support the circular 13th century font. Set onto a 17th century table is an older altar-slab with consecration crosses. The altar rails and the pulpit with a tester and reading desk are also 17th century. On a tomb-chest are recumbent effigies of William Stratford and his wife Ann Walwyn, d1590. See picture on page 10.

FARMINGTON   *St Peter*   SP 137154

The north aisle was rebuilt in the 19th century but it retains an arcade of three bays of pointed arches with scalloped capitals on circular piers dating from c1200. The chancel arch with three orders of shafts and chevrons and the south dooway with more chevrons and a tympanum with a diaper pattern are Norman. In the chancel south wall are two mid 13th century windows with plate tracery and an older blocked lancet. The west tower and east window are 16th century, and the piscina has the initials of a rector of that period. The porch is 14th century, although restored. The altar rails and several brass memorial inscriptions date from the 17th century, and the font is of 1784. Other monuments include a ledger stone to Mary Eykyn, d1729.

Farmington Church

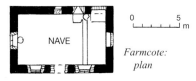

Farmcote:
plan

FORTHAMPTON   *St Mary*   SO 859325

Over the south doorway is a Norman hood-mould with beast-head stops and a grotesque head keystone. The diagonally buttressed west tower is early 14th century. The north aisle is an addition of 1847, the south porch is also 19th century, and the chancel was mostly rebuilt in 1869, although it retains an original stone altar. At the west end are some 16th century pews with linenfold panels. There is a tablet with a skeleton to John Rasteil, d1631.

Frampton-on-Severn Church

FRAMPTON-ON-SEVERN   *St Mary*   SO 744070

The nave and north and south aisles with four bay arcades date from about the time of the consecration recorded in 1315. The chapels at the east end of each aisle are 15th century and the east end of the chancel was added during a restoration of 1868-70. The chapel east windows have cusped tracery with quatrefoils and embattled transoms, and hoodmoulds with angel-stops. Several windows have old glass, one in the north aisle having the Berkeley arms. There is a lead font of the 1160s or 70s. The pulpit is of 1622 and the royal arms are of 1756. An 18th century hatchment shows the sixteen quarterings of the arms of the Clifford family. Their arms are also said to have once appeared on the shields of a recess containing an effigy of a lady of c1330. Of about the same date are the effigies of a knight and a small figure of a man in civilian dress. There are tablets to Anthony Clifford, 17th century, John Clifford, d1684, Ann Wade, d1687, William Clutterbuck, d1727, Samuel and James Pearce, d1798 & 1789.

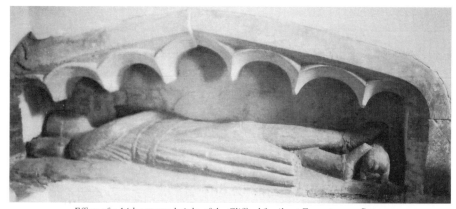

Effigy of a 14th century knight of the Clifford family at Frampton-on-Severn

St Mary de Crypt, Gloucester   *Remains of Frocester Old Church*

FRETHERNE   *St Mary*   SO 734091

This is a fine and richly furnished Victorian church of 1846-7, designed by Francis Niblett, with two south chapels added in 1857-9. There is a richly crocketed spire with flying buttresses on the north porch-tower. The only older relics are hatchments of the Darell family and a series of 13th century coffin lids with incised foliated crosses.

FROCESTER   *St Andrew*   SO 7710

All that remains of the medieval church of St Peter is a south porch and a tower of 1849, the rest having been demolished in 1952. This church had become ruinous and was replaced by a building which originally stood at Frocester Court but was moved to a new site, probably in 1637, the date that appears on it. This building was in turn mostly rebuilt in the late 19th century, after services had transferred back to the rebuilt older church. in the later church are a Jacobean pulpit and a font bowl of c1680.

GLOUCESTER   *St Catherine*   SO 845190

Nothing now remains of the medieval church or of its successor of 1868 on a different site, the existing building in London Road NE of the city centre being 20th century. Also along London Road (but further west) are the 13th to 14th century chapel of the former leper hospital of St Margaret and St Sepulchre and the late 12th century chancel of the chapel of the leper hospital of St Mary Magdalen. The latter has several 17th and 18th century tablets and an effigy of a lady of c1290 said to have come from the chapel of Kyneburgh by the south gate of the city walls, which was demolished c1816.

GLOUCESTER   *St John the Baptist*   SO 832187

Except for the 14th century SW tower and spire this classical style aisled church with round-arched windows and a fine east end with a Venetian window and fluted Doric pilasters is all of 1732-4. Original features are the ceilings, the panelled dado around the whole of the interior, the three-decker pulpit, and the reredos and altar rails. A medieval chest survives, plus fragments of two brasses. There are several 18th century tablets, plus a monument with a half-length effigy of Thomas Price, d1678.

GLOUCESTER   *St Mary de Crypt*   SO 831184

The cruciform plan is of Norman origin, although the only actual 12th features are arches in part of the crypt. The west doorway with a tympanum depicting the Agnus Dei is a 19th century reproduction. Of the 13th century are the north doorway, the west responds of the arcades and the lancets in the south chapel, including one group of three with trefoil heads. This chapel has a 14th century east window, and there are others in the aisles, Rebuilding probably during the period when Henry Dene was prior of Llanthony from 1461 to 1501 provided the three bay arcades with cruciform piers, the liernevaulted tower and the chancel of three bays with a tall east window, triple sedilia and a piscina on the south and a single sedile and an Easter Sepulchre on the north side. Also of that period are the stone screens between the chancel and chapels and the rib-vaulted two storey porch. The clerestory and roof of the chancel are 16th century. The parapets and pinnacles of the tower were removed in 1908, being unsafe. The recessed monument in the south chapel may be of Richard Manchester, d1460. A tomb chest of Sir Thomas and Lady Bell, d1567, has lost its effigies. The brasses of John and Joan Cooke, d1529, are much restored. Brasses of William Henshaw, d1519, and his two wives have come from St Michael's church. A late 15th century slab with an incised cross commemorates Isabel Pole, whose husband was once the mayor. Other monuments include a bust of Mayor Richard Lane, d1667, a kneeling effigy of Daniel Lysons, d1681, and a mourning figure to a Mrs Snell, d1746.

Gloucester: St John the Baptist's Church

Gloucester: St John the Baptist's Church

Gloucester: St Mary de Crypt Church

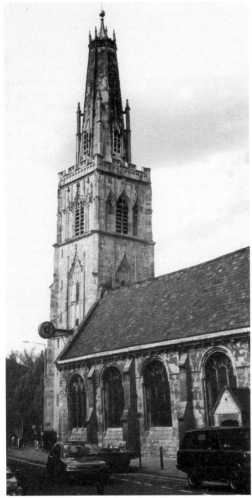

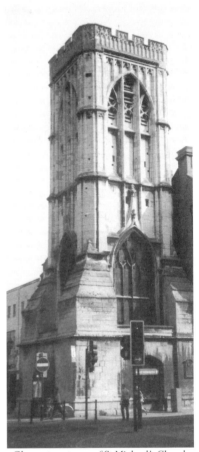

Gloucester: tower of St Michael's Church

Gloucester: St Nicholas' Church

GLOUCESTER *St Mary de Lode* SO 829189

The church has a nave of 1826, a 14th century central tower over a Norman west arch and a 13th century east arch leading to a 13th century chancel with quadripartite vaulting springing from clustered wall-shafts. The effigy of a priest under a mutilated arched recess in the chancel north wall may be William de Chamberlayne, d1304.

GLOUCESTER *St Michael* SO 831185

Just the lierne-vaulted tower of the 1460s remains standing at the central crossroads of the city. The upper stages have canted corners and panelling with two main mullions rising up through the bell-stage. The south aisle and its arcade and the east end were rebuilt in the 1650s. There was further rebuilding to this irregularly planned building in 1740 and the 1770s. A more regularly planned church of 1851 was removed in 1956.

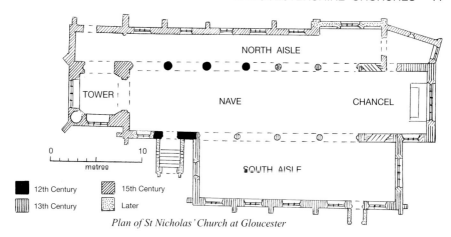

NORTH AISLE

TOWER

NAVE

CHANCEL

SOUTH AISLE

0   10

metres

■ 12th Century ▨ 15th Century

▥ 13th Century ▦ Later

Plan of St Nicholas' Church at Gloucester

GLOUCESTER *St Nicholas* SO 829188

This church in Westgate Street now in the care of the Churches Conservation Trust has a lierne-vaulted 15th century west tower with a coronet, pinnacles and ball-finial of 1783 now crowning the truncated spire, which had by then developed a severe lean. Two arches of the north arcade and the south doorway with a tympanum depicting the Agnus Dei are early 12th century. Three more of the arches are early 13th century and the sixth at the west end is later. On the south side there is a porch with a wide 13th century aisle with a four bay arcade east of it. The arcade piers are circular and have stiff-leaf capitals. Of the later medieval period are the windows set in older surrounds in the south aisle, the north aisle windows, the chancel east window and the squints. A bronze 14th century knocker with a grotesque head holding a ring in its mouth is now in a local museum. There are painted effigies on a tomb chest of Alderman John Walton and his wife, d1626, and there is a half-effigy of the young divine Richard Green, d1711.

Door knocker from St Nicholas, Gloucester

Church of St Mary de Lode at Gloucester

Great Barrington Church

GREAT BARRINGTON   *St Mary*   SP 205135

Of a large and fine Norman church there remains only the chancel arch with chevrons and billet moulding set on round jamb shafts with scalloped capitals. The four bay arcade of two chamfered orders on round piers with water-holding bases is early 13th century. Otherwise the nave and north aisle, and the font and the ashlar-faced top of the west tower, are work of c1511 with a clerestory and square-headed windows. A north porch of this period was rebuilt along with the chancel in the restoration of 1880. Monuments include those of the Bray children, d1720, James Stephens, d1692, a bust of Mary, Countess talbot, d1787, and an effigy of Captain Emund Bray, d1620.

Great Barrington Church

Chancel Arch at Great Washbourne   *Great Washbourne Church*

GREAT RISSINGTON   *St John the Baptist*   SP 195171

The arches under the 15th century central tower are late 12th to early 13th century, the north and south arches being lower and slightly later than the others. The arches have traces of 14th century wall paintings. The north transept with its square-headed east window is 14th century, and the south transept has a reset piscina of that period. The blocked north doorway with decorated spandrels and two adjacent windows, plus the font, are of c1500, but much of the nave and south transept and the whole of the chancel were rebuilt in 1873, and the north transept north window is probably 18th century. There is monument with minuture figures to John Barnard, d1621.

GREAT WASHBOURNE   *St Mary*   SO 987345

The Early Norman nave has original north and south doorways, the latter with a tympanum with a Maltese cross, pellets between rays, dogtooth and six-leaved roses and stars. The north wall has one deeply splayed window and there is a small chancel arch with chamfered imposts. It is flanked by two later trefoil-headed squints. The chancel has one 15th century south lancet and a bell-turret over its west end. An inscription records the rebuilding of the east end by James Cartwright in 1642. There are traces of 12th century wall-paintings. There are royal arms of George III and a two decker pulpit of about the same period.

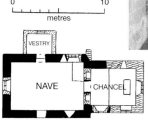

*North doorway at
Guiting Power*

Great Washbourne: plan

Great Witcombe Church

GREAT WITCOMBE *St Mary* SO 911149

The chancel arch with shafts with scalloped capitals is Late Norman, and there are two Norman windows which have been enlarged externally. The 15th century north aisle has square-headed windows with complex tracery with fragments of original glass, and an arcade of three bays with octagonal piers. The west tower with pilaster corner buttresses was completed in 1752, the date of the sundial upon it. The south porch is also probably of that period. What is now a passage between the aisle and chancel originally gave access to the rood-loft, which was lighted by small windows. The rood-beam still remains and above it the wagon rooof becomes a canopy with moulded ribs and bosses. There are royal arms of George III. The pulpit is made up of 17th century panels and banisters from the old manor house now succeeded by Witcombe Park.

GRETTON *Dedication Unknown* SP 006305

The existing church is of 1868 and of the medieval church elsewhere there remains only the 15th century diagonally buttressed west tower with a hipped roof.

GUITING POWER *St Michael* SP 096245

A north transept was added in 1820 and a south transept in 1844. The south wall of the latter has a reset Norman doorway with a new tympanum under an arch of three orders with roll and chevron mouldings. There is a second Norman doorway with chevrons, billets and stars in the nave north wall (see page 79). The chancel has a 13th century priest's doorway and adjoining low-side window. It also has a cinquefoil-headed piscina but was otherwise mostly rebuilt in 1903. The diagonally buttressed west tower and parts of the nave roof and also the octagonal font with quatrefoils are 15th century. There is a tiny old coffin for an infant. There are royal arms of George III. See page 79.

Guiting Power Church

Wall painting at Hailes

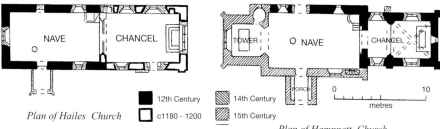

Plan of Hailes Church

12th Century c1180 - 1200 14th Century 15th Century

Plan of Hampnett Church

HAILES *Dedication Unknown* SP 050301

The nave probably dates from the 1130s, whilst the chancel of the same width is Late Norman. The east window with reticulation and the trefoil-headed lancets in the side walls are 14th century. There is also a trefoil-headed double piscina and a priest's doorway cut through former sedilia. The chancel has a plastered wagon roof and the nave roof has braced kingpost trusses and a frame to carry timber-framed belfry. Wall paintings depict monsters, saints and the devices of Richard, Earl of Cornwall, King of the Romans and Eleanor of Castile, wife of Richard's uncle King Edward I. Their devices also appear on tiles. The octagonal font on a shaft with four claws probably dates from the 1250s. On the chancel floor is a cross-slab of c1380. The 15th century screen has part of a parclose screen adjoining on the south, suggesting that there was a nave altar. The choir stalls, panelling, altar table, pulpit and one box pew are 17th century, and there are late medieval pews in the nave.

HAMPNETT *St George* SP 100158

The Norman church had a nave, a central tower over a choir with arches of two orders with chevrons, and a vaulted sanctuary. The latter has an east wall with pilaster buttresses and a small window, and the nave has a two original windows and a blocked doorway with a diapered tympanum. In the 15th century the nave was widened to the south, given a new font and a rood staircase provided to the south of the chancel arch. A south porch and a diagonally buttressed west tower were added. The door of that period has an original iron closing ring. The chancel wall paintings are of c1871.

Capital of arch under central tower at Hampnett

Norman tympanum at Hampnett Church

Hardwicke Church

Bellcote at Harescombe

HARDWICKE   *St Nicholas*   SP 794124

The south doorway, the SW tower and the font with an arcaded bowl are 13th century. The tower parapet is later medieval. The three bay south arcade was rebuilt c1840 and the north aisle of 1876 has an arcade which copies it. There is a classical arch between the 13th century chancel and the south chapel, which has a 14th century east window. A chancel south window set over two piscinae now looks into the chapel. There are several late 16th and 17th century tomb chests to members of the Trye family, one of them having effigies of John, d1591 and his son Peregrine, the latter a small figure.

HARESCOMBE   *St John the Baptist*   SP 837103

Most of this small building existed before the consecration recorded in 1315. Some of the trefoil-headed lancets have been renewed. The piscinae in the nave and chancel have cinquefoiled heads and there is also a credence shelf. The font bowl is set upon thirteen clustered shafts with bell-shaped capitals. Over the chancel arch is a bellcote in the form of a small octagonal spire supported on walling to north and south and brackets to east and west. It has a small octagonal pinnacle on each side.

HARESFIELD   *St Peter*   SO 810104

There is a sheela-na-gig on the NE corner, but otherwise the north side seems to have been refaced during the restoration of the 1840s. Over the north doorway is a restored Norman tympanum. The west tower with a NE stair turret and clasping buttresses on the west corners, a spire, and a tierceron vault inside is 14th century. Several windows represent 14th century types, including one ogival-headed lancet in the sanctuary which forms a separate compartment beyond the choir. The east window is late 14th or 15th century. There are north and south porches and the nave has an old roof with trussed collar-beams. The lead font with cusped arcading and vertical shafts with buttons may be 17th century. Monuments include two female effigies of c1320, one under a ogival-arched recess, and tablets to Blanche Quiatt, d1592, John Rogers, d1670, John Rogers, d1683, John Rogers, d1698, and John Niblett, d1794.

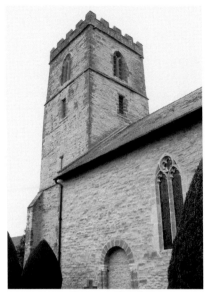

Hartpury Church

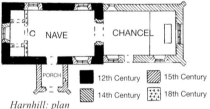

NAVE | CHANCEL

PORCH

■ 12th Century   ▨ 15th Century

▨ 14th Century   ▨ 18th Century

Harnhill: plan

Haresfield Church

HARNHILL   *St Michael*   SP 070004

The south doorway has a Norman tympanum showing St Michael and the Dragon. The porch in front is 13th century, but the trefoil-headed niche in its east wall is 15th century. The chancel arch and one north lancet may be 13th century, otherwise the chancel with a three light east window with old glass and diagonal corner buttresses is 14th century. In 18th century an arch was inserted to support a small slate-sided tower built against the former bellcote. it has a dragon weather-vane. The plain font is probably 14th century. A former altar table is 17th century, and the pulpit is of 1785.

HARTPURY   *St Mary*   SP 803246

A 14th century tower has been added against the west wall of the Norman nave, in which survives an original window. On the south side there is a Norman doorway and some herringbone masonry. A new east end to the chancel was provided in the early 14th century, when the nave gained several new windows, in which remain fragments of old glass. The octagonal font with pairs of quatrefoils and tracery panels on the stem is late 14th century. It has a cover dated 1668. The pulpit is Jacobean. There are monuments to Ann Webb, d1701 and Thomas Pulton, d1778. Recently relocated in the churchyard is a fine example of a 19th century bee-shelter. See plan on page 84.

Hasfield Church

Hawling Church

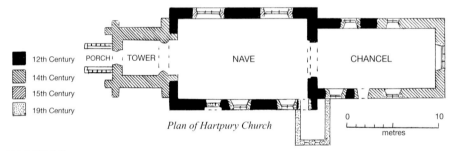

- ■ 12th Century
- ▨ 14th Century
- ▧ 15th Century
- ▦ 19th Century

PORCH   TOWER   NAVE   CHANCEL

0 — 10
metres

Plan of Hartpury Church

HASFIELD   *St Peter*   SO 827277

The tower has a later medieval top stage with gargoyles on an older base, and a NE stair-turret. On the south side is a shield dated 1719. The nave has a 14th century wagon-roof and contains a Norman font, medieval bench ends and a pulpit composed of Jacobean panels, but the 14th and 15th century windows have mostly been renewed. The four bay arcade has octagonal piers with bands of ballflowers above the capitals, but the aisle was entirely rebuilt in 1850. The monuments include a tablet to Henry Brown, d1620, and a tomb chest of Dorothy Pauncefoote, d1568.

HATHEROP   *St Nicholas*   SP 154051

Only a recumbent effigy of an early 14th century priest survived the total rebuilding of the church in 1854 to a design by Henry Clutton for Lord de Mauley.

HAWLING   *St Edward*   SP 063230

The south doorway is partly Late Norman. The west tower is late 14th or 15th century and there is a window of that period nearby in the south wall. The church was otherwise mostly rebuilt in the 1760s, with windows of two lights on the north side and a Venetian east window. The font and pulpit also date from the time of the rebuilding.

Tomb chest outside Hazelton Church

Hempsted Church

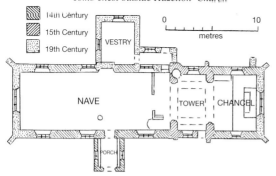

Legend:
- 14th Century
- 15th Century
- 19th Century

0 — 10 metres

VESTRY

NAVE

TOWER | CHANCEL

PORCH

Plan of Hempsted Church

Effigy at Hempsted Church

HAZELTON *St Andrew* SP 080183

The Norman chancel arch (much restored) and the south doorway have chevrons and scalloped capitals on the shafts. The chancel is mostly rebuilt but it retains two shafts in the east corners for an intended rib-vault. Of the 13th century are one trefoil-headed lancet west of the 14th century porch and the octagonal font with an arcade of tre-foil-headed panels. The west tower and several windows, plus the cinquefoil-headed niche in the porch east wall are 15th century. The sill of the niche has been formed from an earlier graveslab with a fine incised cross. Another cross-slab of this type lies in the churchyard, along with a stone coffin and a table-tomb of 1644.

HEMPSTED *St Swithun* SO 814170

In 1885 the 14th century chancel was given a north vestry and a new east window, whilst the nave was lengthened and the windows mostly restored or rebuilt. The nave roof retains original embattled tie-beams with pierced spandrels, ribs with bosses, and carved heads. A head with a mitre is said to represent Henry Dene, Prior of Llanthony until his promotion in 1501 to the archbishopric of Canterbury. Much of the church was built in his time, with a narrow central tower with gargoyles and tracery panels. The north window of the crossing has stained glass showing another mitred head. A brass depicts the children of Arthur Porter, 1548, and there is a painted recumbent effigy of Judge Richard Atkyns, d1610. There is a good Baroque monument to Thomas Lysons, d1713. There are several other tablets, notably that of Daniel Lysons, d1789. Outside is a table tomb of John Freeman, a Royalist killed during the 1643 siege of Gloucester.

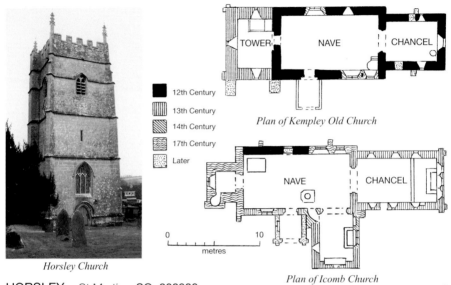

12th Century
13th Century
14th Century
17th Century
Later

Plan of Kempley Old Church

TOWER NAVE CHANCEL

NAVE CHANCEL

0 10
metres

Horsley Church

Plan of Icomb Church

HORSLEY *St Martin* SO 838980

The church served a small Augustinian priory which lay to the south. It is now a cruciform building of 1838-9 except for the 15th century west tower with crocketed pinnacles and a stair-turret on the north side. At noon the shadow of the tower's west wall falls onto a stone to the north. The transepts contain old glass, there are several tablets to the Davis family of clothiers, and a socket of a churchyard cross lies near the gate.

ICOMB *St Mary* SP 214227

The nave north wall has a blocked Norman north doorway and two windows of about the same period as the early 17th century saddleback-roofed tower. The south doorway with keel mouldings and shafts with floriated capitals are 13th century, as is the fine chancel with three lancets on each side and a triplet of lancets with detached shafts in the east wall, which has clasping corner buttresses. On the south side are a piscina and a priest's doorway. The south transept has a 14th century cinquefoil-headed piscina and an arch into it with roll-mouldings and clustered shafts. A passage connecting the transept with the nave is 15th century. The octagonal font with quatrefoils is also 15th century. A tomb chest of Sir John Blaket, d1431 (who rebuilt Icomb Place) has his figure in armour on top and several other figures in canopied niches along the side. There is also a tablet to William Cope, d1691.

KEMBLE *All Saints* ST 990970

The 13th century west tower has corner pilasters and a spire of 1824. Four 13th century cross-slabs have been used later to repair the SE buttress. Also 13th century are the south doorway and the outer arch of its porch, and a piscina and trefoil-headed sedlia removed to here from a church at Ewen. There is also a tomb recess of c1320, and a font of later in the 14th century. The church was mostly rebuilt in the 1870s by Medland and Son, when the north aisle was added. The organ and its case are of c1788. The monuments include a Purbeck marble effigy of a knight of c1290, and tablets to Elizabeth Coxe, d1783, and Ann Coxe, d1790.

Tomb and effigy in Icomb Church

13th century chancel at Icomb

KEMPLEY   *St Mary*   SO 666291

Superseded by a church of 1902-3 away to the east, the Norman church was declared redundant in 1976 and is now in the care of English Heritage. The tunnel-vaulted chancel and the nave each have one small Norman window on the north side and there is a slightly enlarged east window with a roll-moulding. There are chevrons on the chancel arch of two orders. More chevrons appear over a pellet band and a Tree of Life tympanum over the south doorway of c1150. The west window and the plain former doorway now giving access to a 13th century tower may be earlier 12th century work and the open oak roof has been dated to the period c1120-50, making it the earliest of its type in NW Europe. It has fifteen trusses with upper and lower collars. The tower now has a pyramidal roof in place of a spire taken down in 1824. See back cover picture & p15.

The church lacks foundations and has had to be stablised to protect the wall-paintings, many of them as old as the roof, and of European-wide importance. The chancel vault has Christ in the act of benediction set in a triple mandorla. There are seraphim towards the corners and towards the chancel arch are St Peter and St Mary, who is crowned. Beneath an arcade are the twelve Apostles. Heavenly Jerusalem is shown over the side windows, in the splays of which are chequer patterns. East of them are pilgrims, perhaps members of the de Lacy family. South of the east window is a bishop and above are roundels enclosing angels with scrolls. The pattern of triangles in the nave side of the chancel arch was the backdrop to a sculpted rood flanked by painted figures of St Mary and St John. On the south side are the Three Marys at the Sepulchre. Nothing remains of a Doom painting set over this composition. The SE window of c1320 in the nave has contemporary painted figures likely to be of St Margaret and St James. Further west is a scene of the Martyrdom of St Thomas Becket with knights in armour of the 1370s. On the north wall is a figure of St Christopher and there is a round-arched 17th century window cutting into a painted 12th century consecration cross. Of the 15th century are the Wheel of Life and figures of St Anthony facing St Michael in a window splay. On the west wall are 17th century texts. See page 6.

Under the tower is a Norman cross. There are 17th century pews and a circular 16th century font. All three Norman doorways have Norman ironwork and the west door has original woodwork as well. There are monuments to Dorcas Lewes, d1672 and Thomas Pyndar, d1722, and there are three 18th century chest tombs near the porch.

Kingscote Church

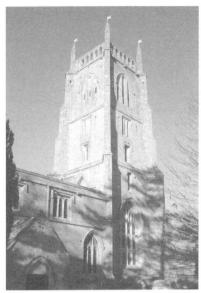

Kempsford Church

KEMPSFORD *St Mary*   SU 161965

The ashlar-faced nave of c1120-30 has four original windows and north and south doorways with chevrons and shafts with spirals and scalloped capitals. There is a 13th century window in the south porch, which faced towards the former castle and is now a vestry. The north porch is of c1520, although its gable was replaced in 1860. The fine central tower with diagonal buttresses, a lierne-vault and a statue niche on the north is probably mid 15th century. The red roses of the dukes of Lancaster appear on the centre of the vault, and the corner shields include those of the de Clares, St Mary's College at Leicester, which may have sponsored the work, and Edward the Confessor. The nave roof, clerestorey and parapet with grotesque figures are also mid 15th century. The west window with cusped intersecting tracery is of the 1330s or 40s. The chancel has an east window of c1300 with a sexfoil in a circle over three lancets. The two bay arcade towards the south chapel is of 1858. One north window has old glass showing the Virgin being taught to read by St Anne. On the nave north wall is a panel from a former west gallery painted with King David holding his harp. On the north side of the chancel is a tomb chest with an effigy of a priest of c1450. There is also a brass depicting Walter Hickman, d1521, with his wife and two sons.

KINGSCOTE   *St John*   SP 819963

Features which survived a heavy restoration in 1851 are the round-arched north doorway, the chancel arch with two plain chamfered orders, the small 13th century lancets on either side of the chancel, and the embattled 15th century west tower with a spirelet over the NE stair turret. The north transept appears to be early 19th century. The screen inscribed Anthony Kingscote 1615 may have been part of a family pew. There are many 17th and 18th century table-tombs of members of the Kingscote family and the porch has an inscription commemorating the marriage of Edward Jenner and Catherine Kingscote in 1788.

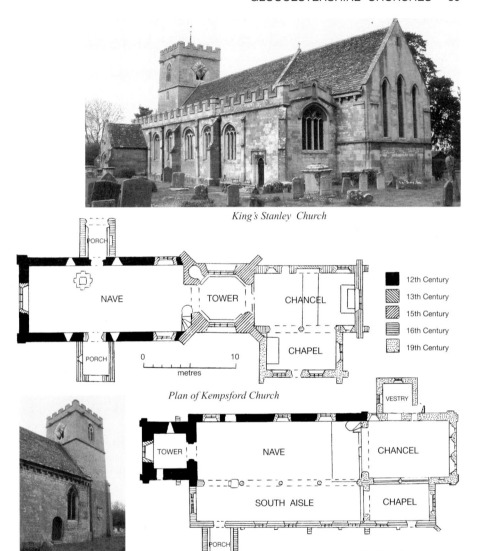

King's Stanley Church

Plan of Kempsford Church

12th Century
13th Century
15th Century
16th Century
19th Century

King's Stanley Church

Plan of King's Stanley Church

KING'S STANLEY   *St George*   SO 810041

The nave north wall with a corbel-table and remains of a doorway and window, and the lower parts of the west tower with pilaster buttresses and round-headed north and south windows are Norman. The embattled upper stage is probably 14th century. There are 14th century windows on the north side and a 16th century south aisle with an image niche over the doorway and a restored four bay arcade. One buttress is dated 1607. Further east are two more arches opening into a south chapel. The oldest tablets are to Richard Clutterbuck, d1714, Obadiah Paul, d1724, Jasper Clutterbuck, d1752, John Holbrow, 1790, Obadiah Paul, d1792, and Sarah Hawker, d1793.

KINGSWOOD   *St Mary*   ST 747920

This church of 1723 has a nave, sanctuary and large north transept. It was altered in 1900. Original furnishings include the font bowl on a fluted base, royal arms of George I, and a chandelier of 1723. There is a Baroque tablet to Persis Webb, d1659.

LASBOROUGH   *St Mary*   ST 822942

A Norman font, a late medieval stone pulpit, and 18th century altar rails and an altar table survived the total rebuilding in 1861-2, when a 13th century piscina was reset.

LASSINGTON   *St Oswald*   SO 796212

The church was rebuilt in 1875 and demolished in 1975. All that remains is a thin 11th century west tower with a 14th century top with a hipped roof.

LECHLADE   *St Lawrence*   SU 215995

When the hospital of St John the Baptist was suppressed in 1473 Cecily, Duchess of York, mother of Edward IV and Richard III, obtained a licence to apply its revenues for the foundation of three chantries in the parish church, which was then being totally rebuilt. It consists of an aisled nave with four bay arcades, a chancel flanked by north and south chapels, and a diagonally buttressed west tower with a spire with rolls up the edges. The clerestory with straight-headed windows and the stone-ceiled north porch were added during the time when Katherine of Aragon was patron in the early 16th century, when the church's dedication was changed to St Lawrence. Fragments of glass with Yorkist badges in the clerestory may be earlier. The nave and aisles are embattled with pinnacles and there is a sanctus bellcote on the east gable of the nave. The chancel parapet is pierced with bands of quatrefoils in lozenges and circles. There is also a pierced parapet on the north vestry. Over the very flat-arched east window is an image of St Lawrence holding a gridiron. On the NE buttress of the tower is a man's head and hand holding a sword similar to that at Fairford. Ten of the bosses of the fine chancel roof have angels carrying instruments of the Passion. Another shows two wrestlers. The font has lost its original base, whilst the lower part is all that remains of the medieval stone pulpit. There are brasses of the wool merchant John Townsend, d1458, and his wife, and of Robert Hitchman, c1520. Other monuments include those of George Coxeter, d1699, Anne Simons, d1769, Richard Ainge, d1778.

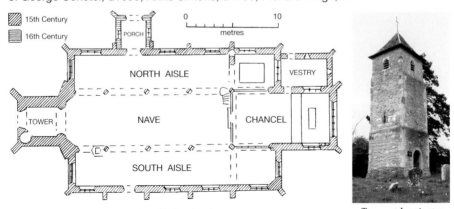

Plan of Lechlade Church   *Tower at Lassington*

LECKHAMPTON   *St Peter*

SO 944195

The rib-vaulted central tower and spire and the chancel are 14th century, although the east window is 15th century. A dedication cross outside is thought to be Norman, and there still survives the east respond of a low Norman south arcade, which was removed c1830. The aisle outer wall is ancient but the rest of the work here dates from the 1860s. A group of worn 13th and 14th century effigies lie outside to the east of the north porch. Another, later, effigy of a priest has been moved back into the church. There are fine effigies of Sir John Giffard, d1327, and his wife. There is a brass of Elizabeth Norwood, d1598, along with incised figures of her husband and eleven children.

Lechlade Church

Effigies outside Leckhampton Church

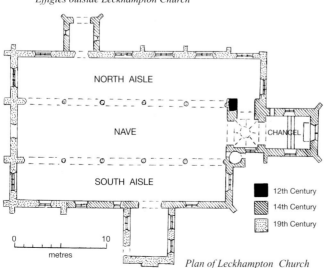

Plan of Leckhampton Church

NORTH AISLE

NAVE

CHANCEL

SOUTH AISLE

0   10
metres

■ 12th Century

▨ 14th Century

▨ 19th Century

Leckhampton Church

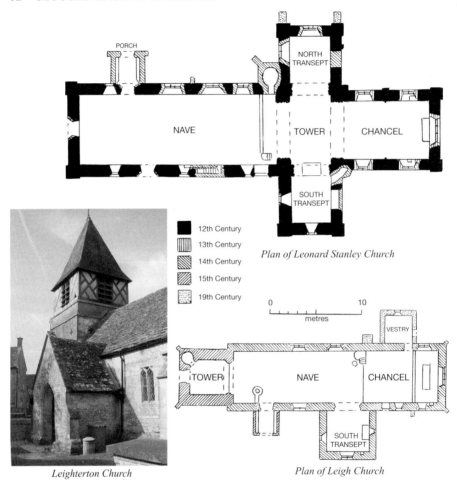

12th Century
13th Century
14th Century
15th Century
19th Century

Plan of Leonard Stanley Church

0   10
metres

Leighterton Church

Plan of Leigh Church

LEIGH   *St Catherine*   SO 866258

The church comprises an undivided nave and chancel, a south transept with a 14th century piscina, a small north vestry, a timber-framed porch, and a late 15th century west tower with the west side faced in ashlar with winged angel stops to the window hoodmould and an image of St Catherine above. The church was much restored in 1885 but retains a good 14th century roof with braced collar-beam trusses and chamfered tiebeams. The octagonal font with quatrefoils with foliated centres is 15th century. It has a 17th century cover. No monuments predate the 19th century.

LEIGHTERTON   *St Andrew*   ST 824911

The 13th century west tower has a south lancet and a 19th century timber-framed belfry with a hipped roof. The nave, south porch and chancel are also 13th century but were heavily restored in 1877, when the north arcade was rebuilt. Unrestored features are the stoup in the porch and the chancel piscina. The octagonal font with suspended shields with the emblems of the Passion is late 14th century.

Leigh Church

Leonard Stanley Church

LEONARD STANLEY *St Swithin* SO 804033

This cruciform Norman church with a wide nave and an equally wide central tower served an Augustinian priory founded by Roger Berkeley in the 1120s. Parishioners used the nave west of where on the south side a 15th century staircase up to a roodloft has been cut through a 13th century tomb recess, and the canons used the rest. Three Norman windows remain on the south side of the nave, along with two doorways that led into the cloister. The crossing piers have pairs of semi-circular shafts with scalloped capitals. The arch in the east wall of the south transept once led to an apsidal chapel. Near it is squint that led through towards the high altar. The chancel was intended to be vaulted in two bays and has shafts in the middle of each side with good capitals depicting the Nativity on the south and Mary Magdalene wiping Christ's feet on the north. There is a stringcourse with chevrons. The tympanum showing Adam and Eve as animals over the aumbry on the south has been moved from elsewhere.

Later additions include the north porch of c1300, the upper part of the tower and its staircase turret, the 14th century windows on the north side of the nave and the nave roof, plus the double piscina and the windows of c1280-1300 with geometrical tracery in the chancel. The font and its cover and the royal arms are early 18th century. There is a 12th century coffin lid with an incised cross and there are tomb recesses in the nave but otherwise no monuments predate the tablets to Elizabeth Rishton, d1761, and John Holbrow, d1780. See page 14.

SW of the church, set across the line of where one might expect the western range of the claustral buildings to have been, is an 11th century chapel, older than the church, and having herringbone masonry, but still in use in the 14th century, when it was given a new chancel with a surviving east window. This building is not open to the public.

Norman capital in Leonard Stanley Church

LITTLE BARRINGTON   *St Peter*   SP 209128

The two bay north arcade and the south doorway of three orders with chevrons and lozenges are Late Norman. Also Norman is the tympanum with Christ in Majesty with angels now reset on the 15th century outer wall of the north aisle. The east wall of this aisle has image niches on either side of a window with fragments of 14th century glass. The 15th century tower lies west of the aisle. There is a niche of c1500 in the east wall of the south porch. The chancel has 14th century windows and the chancel arch is also of that date. It is flanked by a squint. The piscina has a rebate for a door and a groove for a credence shelf. The font is 15th century. There is a tablet of 1702 on the outside east wall of the porch. Inside is a tablet to John Grayhurst, d1730.

LITTLE RISSINGTON   *St Peter*   SP 189200

The two bay north arcade with overhanging scalloped capitals to the piers is of c1190, and the south doorway of three orders with roll-mouldings is not much later. The aisle was rebuilt in 1883, when the nave was lengthened. The 13th century chancel has lancets on each side and a graduated set of three to the east. There is a low-side window on the SW, a trefoil-headed piscina on the SE and an aumbry on the NE. The roof trusses are ancient but the chancel arch was been mostly rebuilt. The nave has one 13th century lancet, a pair of 14th century two-light windows, and a 15th century roodstair in the NE corner. The tower has its SE corner over the apex of the western arch of the arcade, necessitating the insertion of an extra hexagonal pier for support. The large font with quatrefoils with four-leaved flowers is 15th century. A Baroque tablet of 1682 is the only pre-Victorian monument.

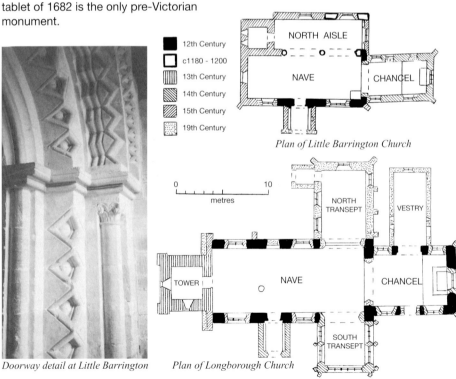

■	12th Century
□	c1180 - 1200
▦	13th Century
▨	14th Century
▧	15th Century
▒	19th Century

Plan of Little Barrington Church

Doorway detail at Little Barrington   *Plan of Longborough Church*

Little Rissington Church

LITTLE WASHBOURNE   *St Mary*   SP 989335

The chancel has one Norman north window with original patterns painted on the embrasure, and the nave west wall retains a set of pilaster buttresses and a string-course. Other windows are 18th or early 19th century. The chancel roof has a braced collar-beam truss, over which is perched a bell-turret. The altar-table, altar rails, box pews, and pulpit with reading desk and sounding board are all early 18th century.

LONGBOROUGH   *St James*   SP 179297

The chancel has a Norman corbel table, and the original chancel arch now lies on the north side in front of the organ chamber. The north and south doorways of the nave are also Norman. The west tower is 13th century below and 15th century higher up, with battlements, pinnacles and gargoyles. The chancel has a 13th century trefoil-headed piscina. The south porch and the diagonally buttressed south transept are 14th century work. The north transept contained a private pew for the Sezincote family and is only entered from outside. There are 15th century windows on the north side of the nave. There are recumbent effigies of a knight of c1325 and of Sir William Leigh, d1631, and his wife. In the north transept is a tablet to John Scott, d1795.

Longborough Church

Little Washbourne Church

Longney Church   *Long Newnton Church*

LONG NEWTON   *Holy Trinity*   ST 910925

This church lay in Wiltshire until 1930 and once belonged to Malmsbury Abbey. The 15th century west tower is embattled, with pinnacles and diagonal buttresses. The rest of the church was entirely rebuilt in 1841 and a north aisle added in 1870. There is a brass to to the priest John Exton, d1503. There are ledger stones with incised arms to Richard Estcourt, d1674, and Grace Estcourt, d1674, and tablets to Jane Henley, d1697, Mary Vaughan, d1717, Ann Millichamp, d1719, and George White, d1783.

LONGNEY   *St Laurence*   SO 764124

On the south side a tower with a 15th century top with battlements and gargoyles set on a 13th century base lies between a good south porch with a panelled arcade and a 13th century south chapel with a 14th century east window and a 15th century south window. The north side has a 15th century timber-framed porch, and 14th century chancel windows. The east window is also early 14th century. The south doorway of c1500 has a four-centred arch with carved spandrels. The nave has an open wagon roof with moulded tiebeams. The south arcade is Late Norman. There are 13th century piscinas in both chapel and chancel. The Berkeley Arms appear on one of the tiles in the 14th century tomb recess in the chancel. The octagonal 14th century font has a panelled and buttressed stem. A monument has a bust of Richard Littleton, d1713, and there are tablets to John Fryer, d1783, and John Fryer, d1799.

LOWER LEMINGTON   *St Leonard*   SP 219346

The Norman nave has a plain north doorway and a more elaborate south doorway with chevrons and shafts with scalloped capitals. On the gable over the narrow and low Norman chancel arch is an original Norman bellcote. The 13th century chancel has a pair of small lancets in the north wall and a two-light east window with a hoodmould. The queen-post roof of the nave and two windows on the south side appear to post date the Civil War, when the church suffered some damage. The original font still remains but has been superseded by an octagonal later one. The combined pulpit and reading desk are 18th century.

LOWER SLAUGHTER   *St Mary*   SP 166266

A 13th century piscina and the much restored Late Norman four bay north arcade are the only parts to have survived the robuilding of 1867. There is a ledger stone to Richard Whitmore, High Sheriff, d1667.

LOWER SWELL   *St Mary*   SP 174257

The original Norman nave and chancel now form a south aisle and chancel to a new nave of 1852 with a chancel of 1870. A few windows had been inserted in the 15th century, when a small porch was added, with a short aisle east of it which was demolished in the 1680s on account of its ruinous state. The Norman chancel arch has three orders, one plain, one with a roll on edge and the third with diapers. Above a double cable is a band of twenty-six carvings, one a sheela-na-gig. The south doorway has two orders, one with double cables and the other with a roll on edge. A tympanum depicting the Tree of Life with a dove on one side is composed of ten stones set together to look like one. The east and west ends have double-chambered string-courses. The font is 15th century but has been recut after being outside the church for a while.

MAISEMORE   *St Giles*   SO 814217

The church was mostly rebuilt in 1869 except for the south porch with an image niche over the entrance and the west tower with gargoyles and battlements. The Norman tub font was recut into an octagon in the 15th century. The pulpit is Jacobean and there are royal arms of George III. There is a tablet to James Pitt, d1784, in addition to several 17th century tablets.

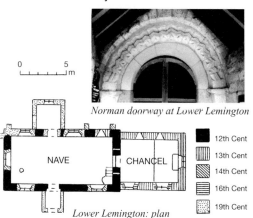

Norman doorway at Lower Lemington

0   5 m

NAVE | CHANCEL

■ 12th Cent
▥ 13th Cent
▧ 14th Cent
▤ 16th Cent
░ 19th Cent

Lower Lemington: plan

Lower Swell Church

MATSON   *St Catherine*   SO 848154

The chancel is of 1852 and the nave is of 1893 replacing one of 1739, which itself replaced a 13th century structure. There are several monuments to the Selwyn family.

MEYSEY HAMPTON   *St Mary*   SP 117001

This is a 13th century cruciform church mostly with lancet windows which is thought to have been built under the patronage of the Knights Templar. The buttresses of the chancel and south walls are original 13th century work, and the nave and transepts have a stringcourse. The south transept east window is a double lancet. The fine east window with ballflowers and the central tower (except for the later parapet) are 14th century. There is a shouldered-lintelled doorway over the west arch of the crossing. The north transept mostly dates from the restoration of 1872-4, when the 14th century tomb recess in the chancel was moved to its present position. There is a squint through the back of it, where there is now a vestry. On the south side is another tomb recess and a fine 14th century set of combined piscina and credence shelf and three sedilia with crocketed canopies. Several windows have fragments of old glass. The lectern has a chain for securing the Bible and the inscription "Christian Jacketts, 1622". There are half length effigies of the physician James Vaulx, d1622, and his wives, and there are other monuments to Margaret Griswald, d1625, and John Jenner, 1787.

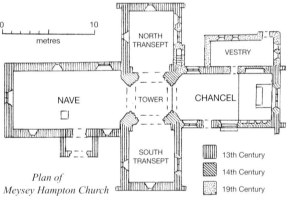

Plan of
Meysey Hampton Church

0 — 10
metres

NORTH TRANSEPT

VESTRY

NAVE

TOWER

CHANCEL

SOUTH TRANSEPT

▦ 13th Century
▨ 14th Century
▒ 19th Century

Minchinhampton Church   *Meysey Hampton Church*

Font at Mickleton

Mickleton Church

MICKLETON   *St Lawrence*   SP 162435

On either side are two bays of Late Norman arches with an early form of stiff-leaf decoration on the capitals. The third bay on each side dates from c1300, when the nave was lengthened and each aisle rebuilt wider than it was before. There is a 14th century west tower with a ribbed and broached spire with four pinnacles on the broaches. A new chancel arch was provided in the 15th century, when a new chancel was added, and also a clerestory on the nave. The 17th century south porch has an upper room with trefoil-headed windows. The porch doorways have imposts, keystones and carved spandrels. The font is of 1661, but looks late medieval. Over the north aisle altar is a 12th century rood figure. There are hatchments of the Graves family and monuments to Thomas Woodward, d1716, John Graves, d1719, Richard Graves, d1729, Utricia Smith, d1744, and Danvers Graves, d1752.

MINCHINHAMPTON   *Holy Trinity*   SO 873008

The central tower with its tierceron-star vault and the north and south transepts are 14th century, whilst the chancel and the aisled nave date from rebuildings of the 1840s and the 1860s. The spire was partly taken down in 1563 and given a stone coronet. The south transept has a large south window with wheel-like rose and ogee motifs. The east and west sides have slender two-light windows between buttresses which support the closely set series of single-chamfered transverse arches crossing scissorwise just below the top. The slab roof over these is visible from within. Under the south window are rich tomb recesses in which are effigies of an early 14th century knight and lady of the de la Mere family, probably Sir Peter and his wife Matilda. There are brasses of a pair of early 16th century wool merchants and their wives, and of a couple shown as cadavers in shrouds (see p16), with their children, the eldest of each sex being depicted as a monk and nun. There are tablets to Joseph Iles, Samuel Sheppard, d1770, and James Bradley, d1762, and some good 18th century table-tombs outside.

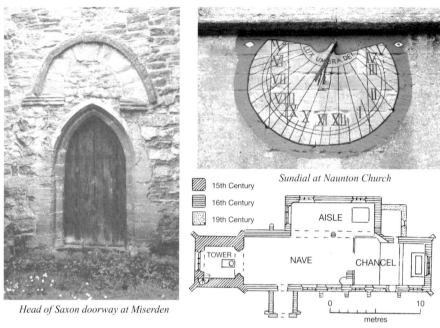

15th Century
16th Century
19th Century

Sundial at Naunton Church

AISLE

TOWER

NAVE

CHANCEL

Head of Saxon doorway at Miserden

0   10
metres

Plan of Naunton Church

MINSTERWORTH   St Peter   SO 773170

The building was entirely rebuilt in 1870 but retains the medieval layout with a wide north aisle and north chapel, the latter now a vestry. The 15th century font has a panelled and buttressed stem. The pulpit is Jacobean. An altar frontal made out of a former cope is early 16th century, although it incorporates 14th century figures. There is a tablet to Charles Barrow, d1787.

MISERDEN   St Andrew   SO 936090

The quoins of the western corners and the imposts and heads of the doorways with horizontal mouldings on each side betray the Saxon origins of the nave. The west tower is Norman, although the upper stage, buttresses and tower arch are 15th century. Norman windows survive in the chancel north wall and reset in the east wall of the south chapel. An aisle added during a drastic restoration of 1866 links the chapel and the south porch. A Norman font is the only ancient furnishing. There are recumbent effigies of William Kingston, d1614, Sir William Sandys, d1640, and his wife Margaret Culpepper, d1644, and there are kneeling effigies of Anthony Partridge, d1625, and his wife. Other monuments include tablets of William Wolley, d1670, William Mills, d1761, Ester Mills, d1782, and the Reverend Giles Mills, d1785, plus a ledger stone to Thomas Warneford, d1717.

MORETON-IN-MARSH   St David   SP 206322

This church was originally a chapel-of-ease to the church at Bourton-on-the-Hill. It was enlarged in 1790 and mostly rebuilt in 1858, resulting in an aisled nave of five bays. In 1860 the 16th century west tower was replaced by a larger structure with an octagonal spire with gabled lucarnes on the sides. There are no ancient furnishings inside.

Naunton Church

Moreton Valence Church

MORETON VALENCE *St Stephen* SO 780098

A timber framed north porch protects a Norman doorway facing towards the moated platform of a former manor house. The arch is roll-moulded and there is a tympanum showing St Michael fighting a dragon. The outer order of the chancel arch also has a roll-moulding, and one Norman window remains in the chancel north wall. There is also a Norman piscina. Along the south side is a 15th century aisle with an arcade of two bays to the nave and a single lower arch to the chancel. Also 15th century are the east window and the embattled tower with diagonal buttresses and gargoyles. Fragments of old glass remain in the aisle east window and there is a font of c1700. There are tablets to John Harris, d1727, and Daniel Willey, d1768.

NAUNTON *St Andrew* SP 112234

The chancel, nave, and short north north aisle with a two bay arcade are all 16th century in their present form. The west tower with diagonal buttresses, pinnacles, and gargoyles is 15th century, as is one window in the north aisle. Still older are a small Saxon cross reset in the nave NW wall, a 12th century corbel-head reset over the vestry east window, and Norman stones used to block a SE window in the nave. Most of the windows have rounded headed lights in square-headed openings. On the south and west walls of the tower are sundials dated 1748. There is a fine stone pulpit of c1400 with canopied panels and pinnacled buttresses.

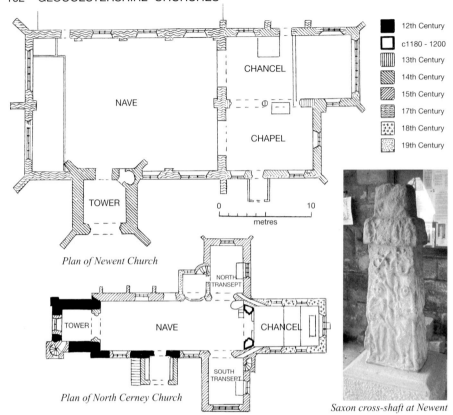

■	12th Century
□	c1180 - 1200
▥	13th Century
▧	14th Century
▨	15th Century
▨	17th Century
▨	18th Century
▨	19th Century

Plan of Newent Church

Plan of North Cerney Church

Saxon cross-shaft at Newent
See also pages 12 & 17.

NEWENT *St Mary* SO 723260

In a rebuilding of 1675-9 following a collapse a wide new embattled nave was built in place of what had been a nave and south aisle. The church was then re-orientated with seating and galleries on three sides facing a pulpit on the north side. The present layout, bringing the chancel back into use, dates from 1865. Two 13th century arches divide it from the south chapel and originally there must have been an arcade of six or more bays. The chapel has a 14th century piscina with ballflowers. On the south side of the nave is a large 14th century tower and spire. The lowest level is a fan-vaulted porch. Here are located several much older relics including a 9th century cross-shaft and an 11th century tablet carved with the name Edred. The pulpit, reredos and font are 17th century, the latter having acanthus leaves on the bowl. The organ case is of c1740. A tomb chest has alabaster effigies of a knight and lady of c1370-85. A brass depicts Roger Porter, d1523. There are tablets to Walter Nourse, d1652, William Rogers, d1690, Elizabeth Nourse, d1757, and Barbara Bourchier, d1784.

NEWINGTON BAGPATH *St Bartholomew* ST 815948

The nave has a blocked Norman doorway of tufa on the north side. The 14th century south doorway has an ogival-cusped arch. The windows appear to all be 16th century. The west tower is rendered with a hipped roof and could be of any date. The chancel was entirely rebuilt in 1858. There is a plain Jacobean pulpit.

North Cerney Church

NORTH CERNEY *All Saints* SP 019078

The Norman church consisted of a low west tower, a nave the same size as at present, and a small chancel. In 1912 footings were seen of a shorter and narrower earlier church here. The south doorway has a fine diapered tympanum and a round arch on shafts with scalloped capitals. There are four human heads on the lintel. The tower has a pilaster NW buttress and several original windows. It was raised c1200 to provide a new belfry and given a new arch towards the nave in the 14th century, when a south porch was added. During a rebuilding from c1470 after a fire the tower was cut down with a new saddleback roof and given a SW corner staircase turret. On the turret is a crudely incised sketch of a leopard. Most of the nave north wall was rebuilt in that period, and a new roof provided. Corbel-heads on the north side are thought to be portraits of Henry VI, Rector William Whitchurch, and Edward Stafford, Duke of Buckingham, executed by Richard III in 1483. There are fine gargoyles below the battlements, with muzzled bears above the doorways. By 1500 transepts had been added to contain a Lady Chapel on the south and a chapel of St Catherine on the north. Both transepts have straight-headed east windows. Beneath the window of the south transept south wall is an incised sketch of a manticore. The chancel walls were rebuilt above the string course in the 1730s, but the east wall and its 13th century window survived until unstability caused its replacement in 1879. The chancel arch is Late Norman. Two windows on the south side of the nave are 18th century.

An outside staircase leads to the gallery of 1754. Under the gallery is a fine 12th century tombstone with a foliated cross in relief. There is an 18th century cover on the 15th century font. There is a very fine pulpit of c1480 cut from a single block of stone (see p13). Stained glass in the Lady Chapel east window has the Yorkist badge of the Flaming Sun, whilst one window in the north transept forms a memorial to Rector Whitchurch. On the roodloft of 1925 is an Italian sculpture of Christ of c1600. There are several old chandeliers and a medieval chest. The chancel has remains of a 14th century tomb. Other memorials include those of Thomas Rich, Master in Chancery, and his wife Anne Bourchier, d1647, Thomas Rich, d1704, and Thomas Tyndale, d1783.

NORTHLEACH   *St Peter & St Paul*   SP 112146

The west tower of c1380-1400 has panelled battlements and upper openings in groups of four with ogival hoodmoulds and pinnacles. This tower was added to an older church which was subsequently almost entirely rebuilt, starting with the nave, aisles and south porch c1400-50. The arcades of five bays have four-centred arches on concave sided octagonal piers. Above is a clerestory and over the chancel arch is a nine-light window. The porch is vaulted in two bays and has an upper room with its fireplace concealed within a buttress and pinnacle on the west side. The south gable has statues of St Mary, the Trinity, St John the Baptist and St Thomas of Canterbury. A similar figure of St John the Baptist appears on the nave east gable. A roof corbel in the Lady Chapel on the south side of the chancel is dated 1489 in arabic numerals. Other corbels depict Henry VII and Elizabeth of York. The chapel is two days long and has a squint towards the high altar. The stone altar remaining in what is now a vestry north of the chancel suggest that this may be a relic of an older chapel. One 14th century doorway remains here leading towards it from the chancel. The chancel has an original stone altar and triple-canopied sedilia plus a pair of carved crosiers set high up.

There is a goblet-shaped stone 15th century pulpit with a fluted stem. The late 14th century font has heads on the octagonal bowl, angels playing instruments, and below the pedestal are demons defeated by baptism. Fragments of stained glass remain in the tracery of the south windows and in the north side of the clerestory. The church has a fine collection of brasses, mostly of wool-merchants with their wives and merchant's marks. Some depict sheep or wool-sacks. The finest are those of a man and wife of c1400 and that of John Fortey, d1459, who paid for work on the clerestory. He has a canopy and marginal inscription with badges with his initials. Another brass shows his father Thomas, d1447 with his wife and her first husband William Scors. Others are of John Taylour, c1485, and family, William Midwinter, d1501, Thomas Bushe, Merchant of the Staple of Calais, d1526, with his wife, the priest William Lander, d1530, Maud Parker, dated 1584, and children of William & Margaret Bicknell, sponsors of the Lady Chapel.

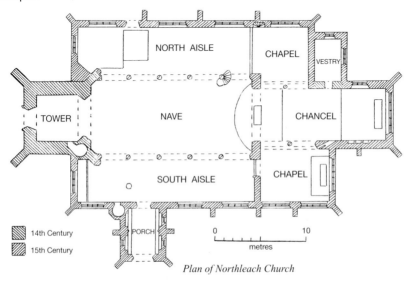

Plan of Northleach Church

Interior of Northleach Church

Porch of Northleach Church

NORTH NIBLEY   *St Martin*   ST 735961

Much of the building was 15th century, the age of the font, but the west tower is dated 1632. The north wall was refaced c1836 and the north porch rebuilt probably in 1861, when the chancel was rebuilt. The south aisle has three light windows, a wagon roof and a tall five bay arcade with octagonal piers. Over the nave is a fine old roof with king-posts, open panelled spandrels and portrait corbels. There are royal arms of 1709 and an oak pulpit of later in the 18th century. There is a kneeling effigy of Grace Smyth, d1609. Her husband John was the historian of the Berkeley family.

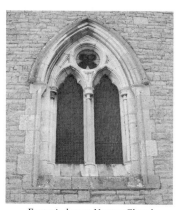

East window at Norton Church

NORTON   *St Mary*   SO 865244

The 13th century chancel has an east window of two trefoil-headed lancets below a quatrefoil, and a priest's doorway. The nave has 14th century north and south doorways with cusped tracery (see page 10). The 15th century west tower has diagonal buttresses, gargoyles and battlements. There is a tablet to Richard Browne, d1636.

Nympsfield Church

Notgrove Church

Saxon crucifix set in later niche at Notgrove

NOTGROVE   *St Bartholomew*   SP 110200

The weathered Crucifix in a niche on the outer face of the windowless east wall is probably Saxon. Backing onto this wall are remains of a red and green painted 14th century reredos. The chancel south wall was rebuilt in 1873, along with the chancel arch and the outer walls of the north aisle, and there is also a 19th century north vestry. The north transept is 14th century, having ballflowers on a window. Norman and other stones are incorporated in the west wall of the rebuilt south porch. The east wall of the porch has an ogival-headed recess. There is a spire on the 14th century tower. The nave east gable also has a sanctus bellcote. The arcade inside is Norman and there is a font of that period with cable-moulding below the rim. One of several old benches is dated 1619 and the pulpit is of similar age. The vestry window has glass of c1300. In the porch is a stone coffin. In the north transept are effigies of priests of the early and late 14th century, the later one on a tomb-chest with quatrefoils on the sides. The chancel contains effigies of two men (one in armour) of c1585-1600, and of a lady of c1630, all members of the Whittington family.

NYMPSFIELD   *St Bartholomew*   SO 801002

Only the diagonally buttressed 15th century west tower with gargoyles and three 18th century tablets high up inside it survived the rebuilding of the church in the 1860s.

Oddington Old Church

Oldbury-on-the-Hill Church

ODDINGTON   *St Nicholas*   SP 235256

The church lies isolated down a lane south of the village and a new church closer at hand was built in 1852, The south aisle of the old church was originally a 12th century nave which retains a simple south doorway. In the 13th century a tower was built east of it, south of a new chancel with a new nave. An arch between the tower and aisle has been blocked up. A piscina shows that the tower base formed a chapel. Here lies one oak bench with carved ends. The south porch is 14th century, as are the windows with reticulated tracery on either side of it. Of the 15th century are the west window, the nave roof and the top stage of the tower. The nave north wall has no windows. In 1913 a Doom painting was uncovered in this most unusual position for such a subject. The octagonal font with quatrefoils is 15th century, and there is a richly carved Jacobean pulpit. The altar table is 17th century and the altar rails are 18th century. Outside, east of the chancel, is a recumbent effigy of Margaret Parsons, d1695.

OLDBURY-ON-THE-HILL   *St Arild*   ST 819882

This isolated building is now redundant. It has a 15th century west tower with low diagonal buttresses. A north porch protects a doorway of c1500. A north window is 15th century and one on the south is 16th century. The chancel has an east window of c1300 with geometrical tracery and head-corbels ending the hoodmould, whilst the rere-arch is cusped. There is a double piscina of about the same date. The box pews and the two decker pulpit are 18th century. The font is probably late 16th century.

OWLPEN   *Holy Cross*   SO 800984

The church was rebuilt in 1828-30, and remodelled in 1874-5, whilst the south porch is of 1897 and the west tower was rebuilt in 1911-12. The only older relics are a Norman font and the eight brass inscriptions from c1600 to 1803 to Daunt family members.

Pulpit, Oddington

OXENHALL   *St Anne*   SO 711266

The church lies on a hillock with wide views to the south and east. It was rebuilt in 1867-8 except for the early 14th century diagonally buttressed tower, which lost its spire in 1972. There is a pulpit dated 1632 but the main object of interest inside is a lead font of the 1160s or 70s with arcading, chevrons, cable, sunk pellet mouldings and six seated figures and six scrolls.

OXENTON   *St John the Baptist*   SO 958315

The oldest features are the 13th century south and north doorways, the latter reset in a 14th century north aisle with a three bay arcade. Also 14th century are the west and south windows and the octagonal font with trefoil-headed panels. In the 15th century an embattled tower was set within the nave upon three arches and the chancel was given a fine new roof. On the north side is a mortuary chapel of c1868. Elizabethan royal arms and commandment boards of about the same period partly obscure the remains of medieval wall paintings, but a female figure carrying a cross can be made out on the south side. The altar table with bulbous legs is of c1600. The choir stalls, choir screeen and pulpit are of 1904-5 but incorporate 16th century parts.

OZLEWORTH   *St Nicholas*   ST 794933

The lower part of the very rare hexagonal tower and the western part of the chancel probably date from c1120. The tower seems to have originally served as a nave and is irregularly planned, the eastern side being much the longest. The upper stage perhaps of the 1150s has a two light window in each face, the central shafts having voluted capitals and cable-moulded necking. In the early 13th century a small nave was added to replace a tiny western porch or narthex. It has a south doorway of two orders with shafts with stiff-leaf capitals and an outer moulded arch with six big cusps with stiff-leaf sprays in the middle of each cusp and in the spandrels. The chancel east end and the south porch are 14th century, but the porch was mostly rebuilt in 1873-4, when the nave was lengthened westwards. The only 15th century contributions are traces of a former roodloft and its staircase and the hollowing out of the SE wall to take a chapel altar. This little church deep within an estate is rarely used for services and since 1982 has been in the care of the Churches Conservation Trust. See front cover and page 5.

Painswick Church

Doorway at Ozleworth

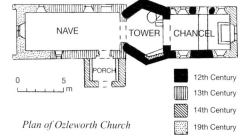

| NAVE | TOWER | CHANCEL |

PORCH

0 5
m

	12th Century
	13th Century
	14th Century
	19th Century

Plan of Ozleworth Church

Oxenhall Church

PAINSWICK *St Mary* SO 867097

The north aisle and the north chapel dedicated to St Peter are thought to date from the 1380s, and the eastern corbels in the aisle are said to represent Richard II and his queen. The plain parapet has large gargoyles. The nave and the north arcade date from the 1480s, and the south aisle was added in 1741. It originally had a Classical style arcade but was given an arcade to match the north arcade in the 1870s, when new windows were also inserted. A Lady Chapel of the 1490s with a cinquefoil-head piscina is now used as the sanctuary. A double squint in the chancel arch north pier indicates that that the east wall of the chancel originally lay in line with that of the Lady Chapel. The spire added in 1632 to the mid 15th century west tower was repaired after lightening strikes in 1763 and 1883. The polygonal south porch is of 1968-9.

The octagonal font dated 1661 bears churchwardens' initials. Hidden behind the organ in the south chapel is a reredos of 1743. The case remains from an organ of c1770. In the north chapel is a chest dated 1621 and a 15th century tomb chest which has been damaged by fire, perhaps during the fighting here in 1644. A new canopy was added after Sir William Kingston was buried here in 1540. Only the indents remain of brass figures of Sir William and his wife. In 1800 the tomb was altered to take the kneeling alabaster effigies of Dr John Seaman, d1623 and his wife removed from the chancel. Still in the chancel is a monument to the Reverend George Dorwood, d1686, and a bust of Hester Knight, d1742. There are other monuments elsewhere to Edmund Webb, d1697, John Webb, d1712, Mary Jacob, d1767, Edmund Wick, d1768, Charlotte Smith, d1780, and William Carruthers, d1790. There is a particularly fine set of many late 17th and 18th century table tombs in the churchyard. Most were the work of the Bryan family, who also built the gatepiers of 1748, which originally had ball-finials.

Pauntley Church   *Norman south doorway at Pauntley*

PAUNTLEY   *St John*   SO 749289

For company the church has only the court, seat of the family of Sir Richard (Dick) Whittington, lord mayor of London four times between 1397 and 1420. The sandstone nave of c1150 has a fine south doorway with chevrons, shafts and a billet hoodmould, and an even finer chancel arch with shafts with grotesque head capitals and double chevrons. The doorway was reset when the south wall was rebuilt in the 1840s. The chancel and south chapel of St George are 15th century and the short diagonally buttressed west tower with a NE stair-turret and gargoyles is early 16th century. The nave has three 14th century windows, near one of which on the north side an older blocked lancet is visible. The windows have stained glass shields of the Whittingtons. A 14th century timber-framed porch protects the north doorway, which is probably 13th century. The door itself has medieval hinges. The Flemish triptych reredos is of c1550. There are brasses of Elizabeth Pole, d1543, and William Pauncefoote, d1616. In the chancel are ledger stones, the late 17th century ones of stone, and the early 18th century ones of black marble. There is also a monument to Anne Somerset, d1764.

PITCHCOMBE   *St John the Baptist*   SO 852083

The church was rebuilt in 1819 and remodelled in 1869-70. The earliest of several tablets is that of Ann Bond, d1766. There are many good table tombs in the churchyard.

POOL KEYNES   *St Michael*   ST 999955

Over the ogival-headed west window of the tower is the date 1775, when the church was rebuilt. The nave and tower quoins are medieval work reset, some having rollmouldings. The tower top stage and the window tracery is of 1845. The chalice-shaped font is of c1700. Female figures and heraldry remain of an Elizabethan monument. There are tablets to Frances Poole, d1644 and the Reverend Thomas Myles, d1683.

POSTLIP   *St James*   SO 999269

NE of the hall is a Norman chapel restored in the 1890s for Catholic worship after being used as a farm building since the Reformation. Both nave and chancel have Norman windows on each side, and there are windows of c1500 in the end walls. There are chevrons, stars, shafts and a billeted hoodmould on the chancel arch. More chevrons appear on the south doorway, which has a tympanum with overlapping fish-scales and one order of shafts with scalloped capitals. A later arch has been inserted and there are two scratched sundials. There are also traces of a former west doorway. The roof is late 16th century. The NW vestry is of the 1890s.

POULTON   *St Michael*   SP 099007

The existing church and its furnishings are the work of William Butterfield in the 1870s but the porch and the SE window incorporate medieval material from the original church which lay half a mile to the SSW at Priory Farm, where there is now just a graveyard with a number of 18th century tombs. This church served a Gilbertine priory founded in 1350 by Thomas de Seymour, which took over an older building. In the present building are tablets to Thomas Bedwell, d1691, and Francis Bedwell, d1764.

PRESTBURY   *St Mary*   SO 970239

The west tower has a top stage with gargoyles of c1400 on a 13th century base with big diagonal buttresses of 1698 and 1829. The arcades of four bays on the north and three bays on the south are late 14th century, built at the expense of a prior of Llanthony, whose house still remains nearby to the NW. The south chapel has a reset double piscina of the 14th century with cusped heads with a quatrefoil above. There are 15th century windows in the north aisle. The 14th century windows of the south aisle were restored in the 1860s by G.E.Street, when the chancel was mostly rebuilt. The oldest monuments are those of Christopher Capel, d1740, and Edward Hotheway, d1754.

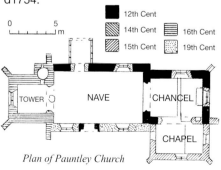

Plan of Pauntley Church

Prestbury Church

Porch and bellcote at Preston by Cirencester

Preston (near Newent)

VESTRY

NAVE

CHANCEL

Plan of Quenington Church

NAVE

CHANCEL

SOUTH AISLE

Plan of Preston Church (near Newent)

PRESTON   *St John the Baptist*   SO 680346

The late 11th century north doorway protected by a 14th century timber-framed porch has a tympanum depicting the Agnus Dei with a Maltese cross. Two windows of the same period remain in the west and north walls. The late 13th century chancel has an east window composed of a pair of trefoil-headed lancets, and single lancets with sedilia below them on each side. There is 14th century glass showing a Crucifixion reset in the SW window of a south aisle added during the restoration of 1859-60. The north vestry was added in 1896. There are Baroque monuments to Richard Robins, d1650, and Anne Robins, d1658, and there is a tablet to Thomas Hanbury, d1708.

PRESTON   *All Saints*   SP 045009

The nave appears to be of Saxon origin and some long-and-short work remains in the western jamb of a blocked north doorway which seems to have been widened in the 12th century. The 13th century south porch has a trefoil-headed outer arch and a trefoil-headed niche in the east wall. The transepts are 14th century additions with windows and piscinae of that period, from which also dates the remarkable bellcote over the 13th century chancel arch. It is of two tiers with ogival-headed openings. Only the surround of the 13th century east window survived a 19th century restoration. The SE window of the chancel has fragments of old glass. The diagonally buttressed west tower with a SE stair-turret is 15th century. There is a Norman font. The coffin-lid by the porch may be 15th century. There is a cartouche of c1725 to the Hamblett family.

QUEDGELEY   *St James*   SO 807142

Only the 14th century tower with a ribbed broach-spire and the adjoining south aisle survived the rebuilding of 1856-7. The roofs incorporate 14th century material. The pulpit and pews incorporate 15th and 16th century panels. Monuments include a brass plate to two daughters of Arthur and Alys Porter, 1532, and tablets or slabs to Richard Barrow, d1562, William Hayward, d1696, and Thomas Hayward, d1781.

Quedgeley Church

Norman doorway at Quenington

QUENINGTON   *St Swithin*   SP 145043

The Knights Hospitaller established a preceptory here in the 1190s but the fine north and south doorways are at least forty years earlier, and result from de Lacy patronage. The north doorway has chevrons, limpet shells and an outer band of lozenges. The tympanum of the Harrowing of Hell shows Christ piercing Satan's bound figure with a cross. There is also a sun disc with a face on it. The south doorway has beakheads continuing all down the jambs. The outer order has ringed pellets. Chevrons border a tympanum showing the Coronation of the Virgin with the Four Evangelists, two seraphim, and a domed temple of several storeys for the Heavenly Mansions. The chancel retains Norman windows and there are pilaster buttresses. The east window is 15th century and there are late 16th century windows in the nave. In 1881 a new west wall and bellcote replaced a thin tower of c1820, and a north vestry was also added. The font is probably late 16th century and has a cover dated 1662. There are tablets to the Reverend George Baker, d1767, and the Reverend Richard Price, d1788.

RANDWICK   *St John the Baptist*   SO 828066

The diagonally buttressed late 14th century tower is the only medieval feature. The chancel was rebuilt in 1825, but now it and the nave are essentially of 1864-7, whilst a double south transept of 1724 was enlarged in 1822-3. The wide south aisle and south chapel are of 1893-6. A vestry of 1904-5 was much extended in 1992. There are royal arms of Queen Anne dated 1711. There are several 18th century brass inscriptions and also tablets to Richard Cooke, d1769, Anne White, d1784, plus several others.

REDMARLEY D'ABITOT   *St Bartholomew*   SO 753313

This church lay in Worcestershire until 1931. It has a big diagonally buttressed west tower of 1738 on a medieval base. The rest of the church was rebuilt in 1855-6. There is a brass to George Shipside, d1609. The numerous tablets include those of Richard Morley, d1773, Mary Morley, d1778, Judith Hicks, d1787, and the Reverend John Morton and his wife, d1785.

RENDCOMB   *St Peter*   SP 019099

The church is mostly the product of a rebuilding begun c1517 under patronage of Sir Edmund Tame after his completion of the work at Fairford. Fragments of stained glass include a shield with Tame's initials. The church has an undivided nave and chancel, a wide ashlar-faced south aisle and chapel extending almost the full length of the building, and a diagonally buttressed west tower which may be slightly earlier. During a restoration of 1895, when the north vestry was added, three piers of a former 13th century arcade were found buried in the north wall. The south doorway and porch entrance have carved spandrels with roses, vines and foliage. Ironwork on the door includes arabic numerals with a date interpreted as 1517. The arcade of three arches and a further two for the chapel has concave sided octagonal piers and flattened four-centred arches. The chancel east window has five lights, that of the chapel has four. There are fine old roofs, with angels playing instruments in the south aisle. The fine Norman font with a key orament and an arcade containing figures of the apostles (one for Judas facing north remains uncarved) came from a chapel at Elmore Court and served as a garden ornament at Rendcomb Park until c1850. See picture on page 11.

Both the chancel and chapel retain original screens with panel tracery and a vine scroll frieze. The pulpit has panels probably from the former roodloft. A panel now forming a cupboard door in the vestry has the pomegranite emblem of Catherine of Aragon. Three of the bells are of the period of the church, two with dedications to St Catherine and the other with royal arms and a dedication to the Archangel Gabriel. An 18th century wrought-iron screen encloses the tomb of Dame Eleanor Berkeley, d1629 in the south chapel. Other monuments include a tablet to Jane Berkeley, d1672, and black ledger stones to Robert Berkeley, d1690 and his wife Rebecca, d1707. Part of a 14th century cross remains in the churchyard along with a 17th century tomb-chest.

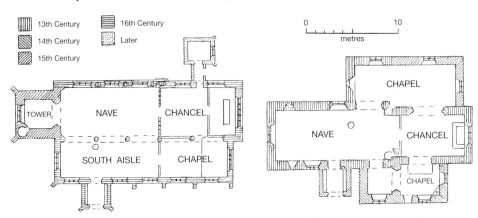

Plan of Rendcomb Church   *Plan of Rodmarton Church*

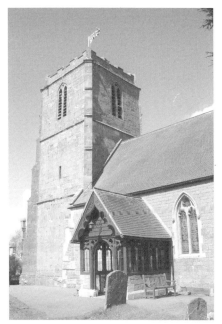

Redmarley D'Abitot Church

Norman font at Rendcomb

RODBOROUGH

St Mary Magdalene SO 844044

Only the diagonally buttressed early 16th century west tower, a pulpit of 1624 and a number of minor 18th century tablets survived the rebuilding of the church in 1841-3. The chancel was again rebuilt in 1895, and the aisles extended alongside it.

Rodmarton Church

RODMARTON   *St Peter*   ST 943981

There are blocked 13th centrury lancets on either side of the nave, and also of that date are remains of a north doorway and a lancet in a north transept which was extended eastwards to form a north chapel in the 14th century. The priest's doorway in the south chapel has an ogival head and of the same period is the south transeptal tower with a spire. The panelled arch between the north chapel and chancel was inserted in the 15th century, when the nave was given new windows, parapets with gargoyles, and a new south doorway with an image niche above a stoup beside it. The door has an original closing ring. Incorporated in the pulpit are several old panels, one dated 1544. There are fragments of 15th century glass in the south chapel windows. There is a brass depicting John Edward, d1461, and a brass inscription to Job Yate, d1668. There are also monuments to John Barnard, d1678, John Coxe, d1730, the Reverend Thomas Coxe, d1779, and the Reverend Thomas Shellard, d1775.

Rudford Church

The lead Norman font at Sandhurst

Plan of Rudford Church

RUDFORD   *St Mary*   SO 780207

The chancel of this Norman church is rib-vaulted in two bays and there is an upper tier of Norman windows to light a chamber above. The chancel arch has roll-mouldings under the arch and a double band of chevrons. There are original west and south doorways with scalloped capitals on the shafts and two orders of chevrons. There are 14th century windows in the chancel south wall, one having a piscina in the embrasure. Also of that date is the octagonal font surrounded by old tiles. Displayed on the north wall is an altar cloth dated 1616 with the name of the donor Rochard Awborne.

SAINTBURY   *All Saints*   SP 117395

The nave has Norman south and north doorways, the latter having a roll moulded arch and a tympanum incised with lozenges. The sundial over the south doorway could be Saxon work reset. The south transeptal tower has a ribbed broach-spire with lucarnes containing Y-tracery of c1300, but an ogival-headed piscina and credence shelf below it cannot be earlier than c1320. Of that later period are two windows in the nave, the north transept, and the whole of the chancel with its double piscina, triple-stepped sedilia and a four-light east window with reticulated tracery. Reset in a south window of the chancel is figure which may be Romano-British or Celtic. The west window, parapet and low-pitched roof of the nave are 15th century, as are the octagonal font with four-leaved flowers and a star-pattern, and fragments of old glass in the east and west windows. The font cover and pulpit are 18th century. The altar rails are 17th century. In the north transept are 16th century benches and a Jacobean altar table standing on a medieval altar-slab. The chancel floor is covered with 18th century ledger stones, There is a brass to Alice Bartlett, d1574, and a tablet to William Warburton, d1649.

SALPERTON

All Saints SP 077199

The nave has a plain Norman north doorway and there is a Norman chancel arch of two orders with shafts with scalloped capitals. The north wall was mostly rebuilt in the 1880s, when a SW vestry was added. The north porch has an outer arch with stops carved with a king and knight with a pointed bascinet of c1400. Of a 15th century tower only its arch towards the nave survived a rebuilding c1700 after it collapsed. Beside the lower arch is a 17th century wall-painting showing Death as a skeleton on a coffin. There are royal arms of George III. There are tablets to Mary Browne, d1758, John Browne, d1782, and Thomas Beale Browne, d1795, and under the tower is a late 13th century grave-slab with an elaborate cross in relief.

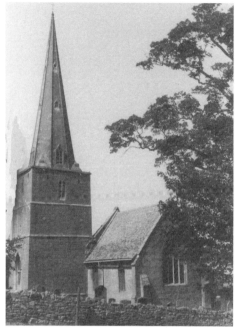

Saintbury Church

SANDHURST   *St Lawrence*   SO 829234

The west tower has a 15th century ashlar top on a 14th century base. The 14th century windows in the nave south wall were renewed in the drastic resrtoration of 1857-8, when a north aisle, south porch and NE vestry were added and the chancel mostly rebuilt apart from a blocked priest's doorway with a four-centred head. The lead font of the 1160s has an arcade of eleven arches with five seated figures and six foliated scrolls. There are two old sundials on the nave SE corner, and a third on the sill of the chancel SW window. There are slate tablets to Hester Gyse, d1673, and Joan Gyse, d1680. There are several 18th century chest-tombs in the churchyard.

Salperton Church

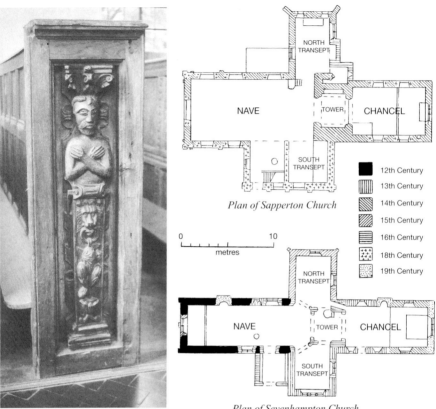

Bench end at Sapperton

Plan of Sapperton Church

0 _____ 10
metres

■ 12th Century
▦ 13th Century
▨ 14th Century
▧ 15th Century
▤ 16th Century
⬚ 18th Century
⬚ 19th Century

Plan of Sevenhampton Church

SAPPERTON   *St Kenelm*   SO 947035

This is a cruciform church with a 14th century central tower with a short broach-spire. The north transept has an ogival-arched 14th century tomb recess and early 16th century windows. The nave and chancel roofs may also be 14th century, but the windows of these parts and the south transept are early 18th century, when a south porch was added and a framed text was painted between the south windows. Reset in the staircase doorway in the south transept SE corner is a Norman impost with a beaded rope moulding. The octagonal font with four circles on each face is 15th century. There are early 16h century benches with linenfolding. Other old woodwork came from Sapperton Manor after it was demolished. In the north transept are an effigy of a knight of the Poole family dated 1574, a tomb of c1500 with quatrefoilos set in a four-centred recess, and a monument with kneeling effigies of Sir Henry Poole, d1616, and his wife. In the south transept is a reclining effigy of Sir Robert Atkyns, d1711. See page 12.

SAUL   *St James*   SO 749094

Two south windows and the nave roof and the ashlar-faced west tower are late 15th century. The north aisle and chancel date from the rebuilding of 1864-5. There is a Norman tub font. The pulpit with round arches and arabesque panels is dated 1636.

Saul Church   *Sevenhampton Church*

SEVENHAMPTON   *St Andrew*   SP 033208

The slender central tower with a tierceron vault set on four arches somewhat east of the centre of this cruciform church was built from funds left by the Worcester merchant John Camber, d1497, to whom there is a brass. Of the same period are the south porch and the remodelling of older transepts with ashlar-work and parapets. The north transept retains a 15th century north window and has a passage squint to the chancel roofed with medieval altar-slabs. The south transept has 13th century triple lancets facing south. The western end of the chancel with single lancets and a round-arched priest's doorway must be early 13th century, whilst the eastern part is a 14th century lengthening, although the east end wall was rebuilt in the restoration of 1892. From the Norman building there remain the three pilaster buttresses at the west end of the nave and the lintel decorated with chevrons over the south doorway. The western corners of the tower have flying buttresses springing from where the transepts meet the nave. There is a chalice-shaped font probably of the 1660s. There are tablets to William Chandler, d1651, Anna Avrigaris, d1651, and Sir William Dodwell, d1727. A series of brass plates commemorate late 17th century members of the Lawrence family.

SHERBORNE   *St Mary Magdalene*   SP 169148

The SW tower of c1300 has a ribbed broach-spire and a vault with eight ribs meeting at a central boss with four heads. A new chancel was built in 1750 but the existing nave and chancel date from the 1850s. John Dutton, d1656, has a shrouded upright effigy of 1661, whilst John Dutton, d1743 is shown in Roman dress. There are other monuments to James Lenox Dutton and his second wife Jane, both d1776, William Naper, d1791, and several others of later date. See picture on page 17.

A cottage at the SE corner of the village incorporates a Norman chapel with two original doorways, one (facing the road) having a tympanum with crosses in roundels, shafts with scalloped capitals, beakheads, and chevrons enclosing pellets.

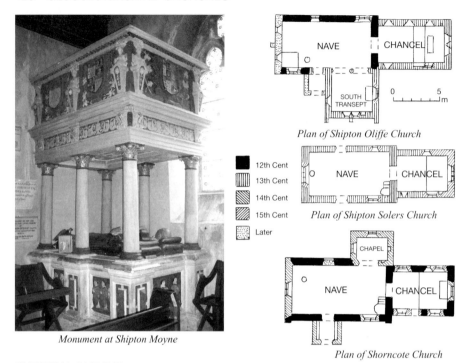

Monument at Shipton Moyne

Plan of Shipton Oliffe Church

Plan of Shipton Solers Church

12th Cent
13th Cent
14th Cent
15th Cent
Later

Plan of Shorncote Church

SHIPTON MOYNE   *St John the Baptist*   ST 892897

The church originally had a central tower. In 1864-5 it was rebuilt apart from parts of the north aisle and porch of c1400, and the Estcourt Chapel dated 1749 on the south side. Members of the Estcourt family with monuments in the chapel include Judge Thomas, d1599, and his wife, and Sir Thomas, d1624, and his wife. In the chancel are three 14th century ogee cinquefoil-cusped tomb recesses with ballflowers. Each has an effigy, one a female, one a knight entirely in chainmail, and the other a knight in mid 14th century plate armour. Other monuments in the aisles include those of Thomas Estcourt, d1746, and Elizabeth Nowell, d1788.

SHIPTON OLIFFE   *St Oswald*   SP 035185

A 17th century window has been inserted into a former Early Norman north doorway with a plain tympanum. The church was remodelled in the 13th century with a new double bellcote with a pyramidal roof supported by pinnacled buttresses, and a south transept and new chancel were added. The latter has three different lancets in the north wall and two east lancets with three orders of roll-mouldings. The chancel arch of that period rests on Early Norman imposts. The chancel south wall has another lancet, a window of c1300 with dogtooth on a hoodmould with male and female headstops, and a mid 14th century canopied piscina. The transept has a piscina and west lancet which are trefoil-headed, a restored 14th century east window, and is divided from the nave by an acade of two bays inserted in 1904. The plain octagonal font is the only 15th century feature. There are traces of 13th century wall paintings on the nave east wall and two 18th century panels of Commandments on the north wall. There is a tablet to Mary Peachey, d1772. See picture on page 5.

SHIPTON SOLERS   *St Mary*   SP 031185

The church was probably consecrated in 1212, an inscription of that date being found over the chancel arch during the restoration of 1929-30. An altar slab then found has been reset upon stone columns. The chancel has one 13th century lancet but the other windows are 15th century when it was lengthened. Other 13th century features are the piscina and aumbry, the chancel arch, the cross over the east gable, and probably the painted consecration cross near a nave north window with a cinquefoiled head. The roofs and the font and the nave windows and doorway are 15th century. The nave walls are painted with 17th and 18th century texts. The oak pulpit is Jacobean. Early tablets include those of Sarah Roberts, d1671, and John Powell, d1734.

Bellcote at Shipton Oliffe

SHORNCOTE   *All Saints*   SU 025967

There is a sundial on either side of the plain Norman south doorway. The north doorway has a fitted arch and shafts with capitals. Its tympanum now serves as a doorstep. The chancel arch of c1200 is slightly pointed and has filleted shafts and a billet-moulded hoodmould. In the late 14th century the west wall was rebuilt, new windows inserted, a double bellcote put upon the nave east gable, and a north chapel added with a piscina with a credence shelf, a niche over the altar and a north window with an elaborate cusped rere-arch. At the nave SE corner is a roodloft staircase. Part of a 13th century coffin lid has been used as the sill of the NW window in the chancel, and another forms part of the nave west window. In the 15th century a small Easter Sepulchre with a cinquefoiled head was set within the deeply splayed embrasure of a Norman window in the chancel north wall. Part of a 13th century patterned mural with eight-petalled rosettes and other motifs remain in the chancel. The east window has glass with the Berkeley arms. There is a Norman tub-font and an old pulpit, whilst the reading desk has 15th century parts. The oldest tablet is that of Richard Kemble, d1733.

SHURDINGTON

St Paul   SO 921189

The thin vaulted 14th century west tower has a tall ribbed spire. Norman are the chancel arch imposts and the mostly renewed north doorway. The north aisle was extended in 1851-2, when the chancel was mostly rebuilt along with the north arcade, and the north vestry and south porch were added. There is a sundial dated 1655 near the 14th century south window of the nave. The south doorway is very low. The 14th century font has an octagonal bowl with quatrefoils and foliage on a round 13th century base.

Easter Sepulchre set in older window at Shorncote

Norman doorway at Siddington

Font at Siddington

SIDDINGTON   *St Peter*   SP 035001

The Norman south doorway has an arch with an outer order of spiral cable moulding and an inner order of beakheads, There is a horned head above and beast-heads on the shafts, whilst the tympanum has Christ in Majesty flanked by St Peter and St Paul. The chancel arch probably of the 1180s is slightly pointed with chevron mouldings and pellets on a hoodmould which curls into beast-headstops. The 13th century north arcade has double-chamfered arches on round piers with moulded capitals. The chancel has early 14th century windows with double sedilia and a trefoil-headed piscina. The east window is 19th century. An arch with concave responds with angel stops with shields with the arms of the Langley family leads into a north chapel of c1470 which forms a continuation of a new north aisle of that period. The organ now obscures the chapel east window, from which c1800 stained glass was taken off for re-use in the church at Cirencester. Canopied image niches flank this window. Recessed into the north wall are two tombs with indents of brasses. A squint through to the chancel is squeezed in under the staircase up to the former rood-loft. The Norman font has interlaced tripartite bands with raised diamonds between a herringbone band and an acanthus scroll at the top and a cable and saw pattern at the bottom. There is a tablet to Benjamin Bathurst, d1767. Outside is a group of four good chest tombs.

Slimbridge Church

SLIMBRIDGE   *St John*   SO 740036

The aisles are faced with blocks of tufa and have round-headed doorways of the early 13th century. There are four bay arcades of that date with moulded and keeled arches set upon piers which are square with chamfered corners and each have four keeled shafts with particularly fine capitals. The early 14th century west tower has a rib-vault and there are image niches beside and above the west window with intersecting tracery. Below the upper niches are blank shields. The recessed and ribbed spire was rebuilt in 1735, and again in 1792 and 1851. Of the mid 14th century is the chancel with elongated reticulated tracery in the east window, triple sedilia and an ogival-headed piscina. Also of that date is the north aisle east window (with 15th century glass) and the two storey south porch. On that side there is a stringcourse of ballflowers beneath the parapet. The other windows in the aisles are probably late 14th century and there are roof corbels of that period. The clerestory was added during the restoration of 1844-6. The lead font with winged cherubs, roses and balusters is dated 1664 and stands on a stone base dated 1634. There are tablets to the Reverend William Cradock, d1727, Robert Awood, d1734, William Davies, d1742, and John Cowley, d1792.

Interior of Slimbridge Church

SNOWSHILL   *St Barnabas*   SP 097337

Only the fine octagonal 15th century font with quatrefoils, flowers and an arcaded plinth survived the rebuilding of the church in 1863. There are old chest tombs outside.

Shurdington: west window

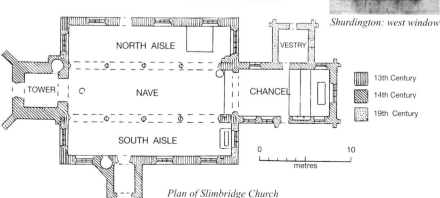

Plan of Slimbridge Church

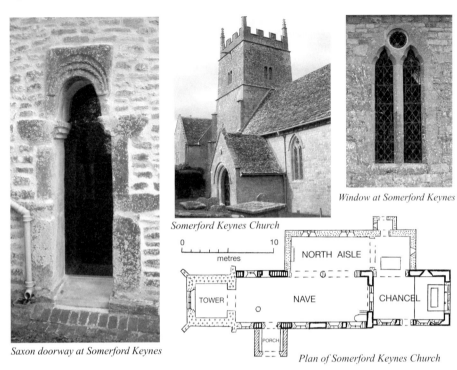

Window at Somerford Keynes

Somerford Keynes Church

NORTH AISLE

TOWER   NAVE   CHANCEL

PORCH

Saxon doorway at Somerford Keynes

Plan of Somerford Keynes Church

SOMERFORD KEYNES   *All Saints*   SU 016956

This church lay in Wiltshire until 1897. It has a Saxon north doorway possibly as early as the 8th century and only reopened in 1968. The jambs and imposts are through stones and the stilted arch is cut through a single stone. It has two bands of cable-moulding on the outer face. Further east is a short aisle with a two bay 13th century arcade with trumpet-scallop capitals on the responds and early stiff-leaf on the pier. The nave SE window has plate tracery and the south doorway may also be 13th century. The chancel has one small north lancet of c1200. The trefoil-headed piscina must be later, and the east window dates from the restoration of 1875-6. There is a squint to the south of the chancel arch, across which is an old screen. There is a reset 15th century window in the west tower of c1708 which replaced a wooden belfry. A Norman font has been altered to fit upon a 14th century hexagonal base with tracery patterns. The round-headed stone with two dragons both biting a ball is probably early 11th century. In the nave SW corner is a collection of 13th century coffin lids with incised crosses. There is a monument with a reclining effigy of Robert Strange, d1654.

SOUTHAM   *The Ascension*   SO 970256

This small Norman church was much restored in neo-Norman style in 1861 to bring it back into use as a private chaped for Edward Law, Earl of Ellenborough, after it had become a barn and then allowed to decay. Genuine Norman features are one small window in the chancel and the north doorway with monolithic jambs and original iron-work on the door. There is a window of c1500 in the chancel. There are three choir stalls with miserichords which are probably late 16th century Flemish work.

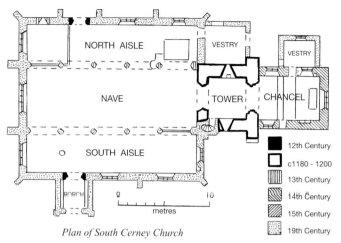

Plan of South Cerney Church

■	12th Century
□	c1180 - 1200
▤	13th Century
▨	14th Century
▨	15th Century
▦	19th Century

Norman window at Southam

SOUTH CERNEY *All Hallows* SU 050973

The central tower has restored Norman windows to north and south and pointed arches of c1200 to west and east of three orders with keeled rolls, keeled shafts and chevrons and rosettes. The spire was never rebuilt after being damaged by lightning in 1857. The four bay north arcade of the early 13th century has double concave chamfered arches on round piers with four shafts which are filleted or keeled and which have crocket or trampet-scalloped capitals. During the restoration of 1861-2 the aisle was rebuilt and lengthened by one bay, a south aisle was added, and the 14th century five-light window with reticulated tracery was reset in the new west wall. The 14th century chancel has ballflowers on the reticulated tracery of the three-light east window (beside which is a wall-painting) and there are ogival-headed doorways adorned with ballflowers in both north and south walls. More ballflowers appear on a piscina set diagonally in the SE corner. The sedilia have arches set upon the head of a bishop. The SW window here contains fragments of original stained glass.

Norman doorway at South Cerney

In a recess under the tower are resin copies of the head and foot of a wooden Crucifix of c1130 discovered in the wall here in 1913. There is a collection of 12th and 13th century cross-slabs. The octagonal 15th century font has quatrefoils on each side. Tablets include those of Thomas Jones, d1768, John Adams, d1789, and Ester Jones, d1791. The big stone coffin outside east of the porch may be Roman or Saxon. There are also two cross-slabs here, whilst west of the porch is a tomb chest with worn effigies of a man and woman of c1370. Beside it is the base of a churchyard cross.

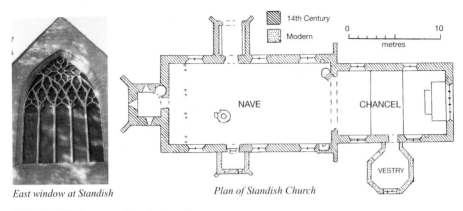

East window at Standish

Plan of Standish Church

SOUTHROP   *St Peter*   SP 202035

The Norman nave has one original window on each side and patches of herringbone masonry. Protected by a late 14th century porch is a north doorway with volute capitals on the shafts and a tympanum with an incised diaper pattern. There are bands of rope and star motifs on the chancel arch, which is flanked by 19th century squints and surmounted by a 15th century squint from the former roodloft. A new chancel was added under patronage of the Knights Hospitaller of Clerkenwell in the 13th century. It has an east window with a lozenge above two lancets and shouldered heads to the priest's doorway and the low-side lights below of the western of a series of three lancets on each side. On the SE corner of the early 14th century south transept is an older sundial, below which a quoin is dated 1747. In the 15th century the nave was heightened and given a new west wall with a three light window and belfry. The bellcote higher up and the neo-Norman windows are of 1895-6.

Font at Southrop

The church has a particularly fine font of c1180 with figures under trefoiled arcading and beaded interlacing. Moses with the tablets is flanked by Ecclesia with a chalice and pennoned cross and Synagogue blindfolded by the pennon of her broken staff. The other arches frame figures of armoured women representing the Virtues trampling over their opposite Vices, ie Modesty tramples on Excess, Patience on Wrath, Generosity on Greed, Temperance on Luxury, and Pity on Envy. The Virtues are named on the arches, and the Vices are named in reverse below. In the chancel is an altar tomb and stone effigies thought to be of Sir Thomas Conway, d1606, and his wife. There are also monuments to Edmund Keble, d1654, and Thomas Keble, d1670.

STANTON *St Michael* SP 069343

Three bays of the north arcade are Late Norman work (somewhat restored) with round piers with trumpet capitals and water-holding bases with spurs. In the 15th century a fourth western bay was added, along with a west tower with a recessed ribbed spire and a new south aisle with heads above the octagonal piers of the arcade. The aisle windows are of the 1890s. The chancel was rebuilt in 1874 but retains a 15th century east window with stained glass figures of saints probably brought here from Hailes Abbey. The south transept has an east lancet of the 13th century and the north transept has 14th century windows and part of an old screen. Both transepts have traces of wall-paintings and squints to the chancel, that on the south being beside the doorway to the staircase to the former roodloft. There is a late 14th century wooden pulpit and an octagonal 15th century font. There are tablets to the Reverend Henry Izod, d1650, the Reverend Henry Kirkham, d1705, and John Warren, d1728.

STANDISH *St Nicholas* SO 801083

Apart from the vestries of c1850 and 1969 the entire church dates from c1340. It has a diagonally buttressed west tower with a ribbed broach-spire with lucarnes, a large and wide nave with a big north porch, and a chancel with an ogival-headed piscina and a five-light east window with intersecting and reticulated tracery combined with a diamond-shaped rose. The nave has roodloft staircase on the south side and a piscina for a secondary altar, below which is a 13th century slab with a female head in relief above a foliated cross within a circle. There are 180 bosses, mostly with foliage, in the panelled roof. The fine pulpit is of1764. There is a tablet to Charles Yate, d1721, and a monument to Henry Winston, d1609, the effigies from which are said to be in Dorset. The churchyard has a very fine collection of late 17th and 18th century chest tombs.

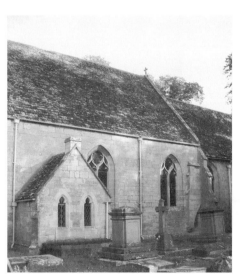

Standish Church

Stanton Church

STANLEY PONTLARGE   *Dedication Unknown*   SP 007301

The whole of the chancel (apart from a reset piscina) and the neo-Norman windows of the nave date from 1860, but there are genuine Norman south and north doorways, the latter having two orders of chevrons, a billet hoodmould, shafts with scalloped capitals and a plain tympanum with a row of dogtooth over the top. There are further chevrons on the chancel arch, which also has shafts with scalloped capitals. One south window is 14th century and the west window is of c1500. The Norman font set upon three rolls was later recut into an octagon. A few old benches remain in the nave.

STANWAY   *St Peter*   SP 061324

The ashlar-faced chancel has a restored Norman corbel-table of grotesque heads and a reset tripartite respond on the north side which suggests vaulting was intended. It has a 16th century NW window. The nave, also ashlar faced, was remodelled in the 1790s and again in the 1890s (when the porch was added) but retains a Norman window above the low 13th century arch inserted through to a west tower with lancets lower down and windows with plate-tracery higher up. The chancel arch also appears to be 13th century. The pulpit is 17th century. There is a coffin lid with a head at the intersection of a cross in relief. Built into the north wall of the churchyard are other coffin lid fragments, a complete stone coffin, the torso of an effigy of c1300, and a number of 12th and 13th century architectural fragments.

STAUNTON   *St James*   SO 781291

This church lay in Worcestershire until 1931. It was heavily restored in 1860, when the chancel was rebuilt and the north vestry and south porch added. The nave south wall has some Norman herringbone masonry. The diagonally buttressed late 14th century tower has a NE stair-turret and a recessed spire. The nave has a piscina next to a 14th century ogival-headed tomb recess. The north aisle and transept at its east end are also 14th century, although remodelled in 1860, and have a four bay 16th century arcade with octagonal lozenge-shaped piers. The 19th century font lies on a 14th century base with heads of a king, queen, bishop and rector. A chest is dated 1742. There are kneeling effigies of William Horton, d1612, and his wife and children.

North transept of Staverton Church

Porch vault at Stinchcombe

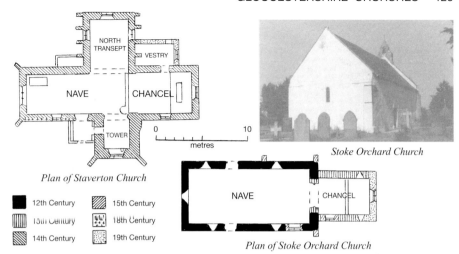

Plan of Staverton Church

Stoke Orchard Church

Plan of Stoke Orchard Church

■ 12th Century   ▨ 15th Century

▥ 13th Century   ▦ 18th Century

▧ 14th Century   ▨ 19th Century

STAVERTON   *St Catherine*   SP 890083

The nave, chancel, and the ashlar-faced north transept with closely space buttresses and south transeptal tower are all mostly 14th century, and a chantry chapel was endowed here in 1345. The tower has big diagonal buttresses, a south window with reticulated tracery, a NE stair-turret, a doorway towards the porch, a piscina and evidence that vaulting was intended. The arch towards the nave with a keystone is dated 1712, when the tower was truncated and given a new parapet, also dated 1712. About that time the nave south wall was rebuilt in brick. The original braced collar-beam roof survives. The brick north vestry is of 1865. The oldest monuments are tablets to Thomas Banester, d1627, the Reverend Henry Wyndowe, d1772, and the Reverend John Kipling, d1794.

Stanley Pontlarge Church

STINCHCOMBE   *St Cyr*   ST 730989

The two storey north porch of c1500 has a lierne-vault with carved bosses and a parapet with quatrefoils with flowers and pinnacles. The tall diagonally buttressed west tower has an open parapet with pinnacles and a spire which was restored in 1884 after being struck by lightning. There are several 18th century memorial tablets. The rest of the church was rebuilt in 1854-5 to a design by J. L. Pearson.

STOKE ORCHARD   *St James the Great*   SO 916282

The Norman nave has five original windows and south and north doorways, one square-headed and having early sundials, the other roll-moulded with original ironwork with beast heads on the door. The walls lean outwards and are covered with wall-paintings of various periods including a rare 14th century cycle of the life of St James of Compostella with twenty-eight scenes. The texts and trellises are 16th and 17th century, and the red fleur-de-lys are 15th century. The chancel arch is 13th century but the chancel itself appears to be mostly 15th centrury. There are old benches, 17th century work in the pulpit and altar rails, and the Norman font has thin intersecting arches.

Stonehouse Church

Stow-on-the-Wold Church

STONE   *All Saints*   ST 685955

The church ranked only as a chapel-of-ease to Berkeley until 1797, and the arms of the Berkeley family appear on 14th century shields of stained glass in the north windows. The tall diagonally buttressed tower with a recessed ribbed spire, the wide nave and the chancel arch flanked by two-light windows are all 14th century. The chancel was rebuilt in a shortened form in 1831, a north vestry was added in 1846, and about that time the south porch was also added. The nave has a roodloft staircase and a piscina, and there is a second piscina higher up to serve a roodloft altar. The pulpit is of 1755, and there are royal arms of George III dated 1789. There are low tomb chests under recesses in the nave and tablets to John Morse, d1728, and John Cox, d1795.

STONEHOUSE   *St Cyr*   SO 880051

The diagonally buttressed west tower with gargoyles is 15th century. The church retained Norman parts until rebuilt and refurnished in 1853-4, hence the neo-Norman north doorway. The north and south chapels and the south vestry were added in 1884. Several minor tablets of c1700 remain under the tower and there is a monument to Samuel Spencer, d1790. Outside is a fine collection of 17th to 18th century tombs.

STOWELL   *St Leonard*   SP 087131

The central tower of this small cruciform Norman church fell, despite attempts to buttress the leaning SE pier, and has been replaced by four gables. The arches below of the 1190s are double chamfered, with waterleaf capitals on the shafts of the west arch. The nave has two plain Norman doorways and a west end of ashlar with a Norman window piercing a semi-hexagonal buttress crowned by a corbel with a beast head. In the 14th century the chancel was given a new east window and an Easter Sepulchre backed onto a patch of external ashlar. The south transept has a west lancet and a trefoil headed piscina of the 13th century, and a south window of the 14th century with an early sundial on its sill. Other early sundials are on the transept SE corner, on either side of the south doorway and on the nave SW corner. The north transept was rebuilt in 1898-9. The plain octagonal font is 13th century. On the nave north wall and south transept south wall are interesting wall-paintings of c1200-20 (see page 132). There are tablets to Lady Annabella Howe, d1703, and Anne Morgan, d1712.

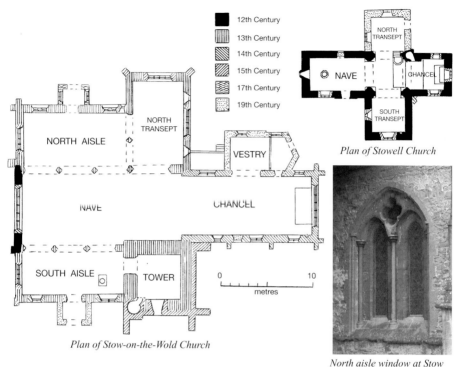

12th Century
13th Century
14th Century
15th Century
17th Century
19th Century

NORTH TRANSEPT

NAVE   CHANCEL

SOUTH TRANSEPT

Plan of Stowell Church

NORTH TRANSEPT

NORTH AISLE

VESTRY

NAVE   CHANCEL

SOUTH AISLE   TOWER

0   10

metres

Plan of Stow-on-the-Wold Church

North aisle window at Stow

STOW-ON-THE-WOLD   *St Edward*   SP 191258

All that remains of the Norman church are pilaster buttresses on the nave west wall, which contains a five-light 14th century window with cusped reticulated tracery. On the south side is an ashlar-faced transeptal tower of the 1440s with panelled battlements, gargoyles and crocketed pinnacles. The base appears to be a recased structure of c1200. The 13th century three bay south arcade clearly allows for a tower and an early arch opens from the aisle into the tower, which has no opening towards the nave. The south aisle was rebuilt, and probably widened, in the late 13th century, having two south windows with plate tracery. Also of the late 13th century are the four bay north arcade with cluster columns with cable and nailhead on the capitals, the north transept with two east lancets, and the wide north aisle with its splendid original doorway of six orders, and windows with plate tracery. There is a two bay arcade between the aisle and the transept. The four-light east and north windows of the transept and the north aisle west window with hoodmould stops of a king and queen are 15th century. The roof corbels are also of that period. The north porch appears to have been added during a restoration of the 1680s, the church having been described as ruinous in 1657, a decade after it was used to confine Civil War prisoners following a battle in and around the town. There is an incised slab to Hastings Keyt, killed in this fight. In the 19th century organ chamber are reset windows from the north wall of the 14th century chancel, in which is a piscina with an ogival head. The east window dates from the restoration of 1854. The goblet-shaped font is late 16th century. In the chancel are monuments to John Chamberlayne, d1667, and John Chamberlayne, d1714. There are also tablets to Margaret Pitman, d1765, and Leonard Hayward, d1780.

Wall paintings at Stowell Church

Stowell Church

Stratton Church

STRATTON   *St Peter*   SP 010040

The nave south wall is Norman with one small window and a tympanum with a Tree of Life and animals set over a doorway of c1500 with a contemporary door. Two later medieval windows were reset in 1849-50 when the nave was extended westwards and given a north aisle, and the chancel was rebuilt. The oldest of several tablets are those of Thomas Nicholas, d1638, and Anne Pitt, d1792.

STROUD   *St Lawrence*   SO 861052

This church in The Shambles, originally a chapel-of-ease to Bisley, was rebuilt in 1866-8 except for the diagonally buttressed west tower with a tall broach-spire. There is a monument with a kneeling effigy of Thomas Stephens, d1613. Numerous other tablets, many of them high up over the tower arch, include those of Thomas Fream, d1664, Richard Field, d1693, Daniel Capel, d1709, Richard Aldridge, d1776, William Knight, d1786, and Robert Hughes, d1794.

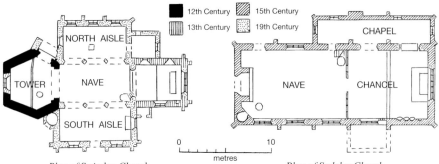

Plan of Swindon Church

Plan of Sudeley Church

Monument in Stroud Church

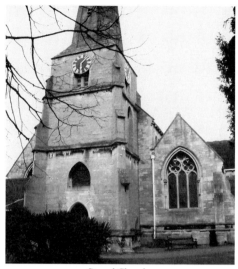

Stroud Church

SWINDON   *St Lawrence*   SO 936248

Only parts of the chancel and the rare hexagonal Norman tower survived the rebuilding of 1844-6. The tower perhaps originally served as a nave and is of irregular plan with the eastern side longer than the others where it has an arch towards a small aisled nave where there was once perhaps just a chancel, although the present nave and chancel layout existed by the end of the 12th century. The tower has a doorway with shafts with cushion capitals facing NE and round-headed two-light belfry openings with cushion capitals on the shafts. The octagonal font with quatrefoils is 15th century and the stone pulpit may be 16th century. There are several 18th century tablets in the north aisle, and under the tower is a tablet to Mary Surman, d1772.

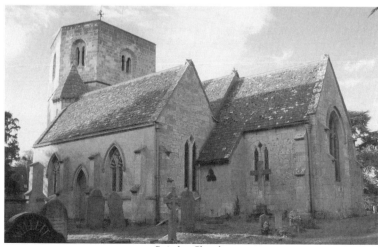

Swindon Church

Interior of Tetbury Church

Sudeley Church

Syde Church

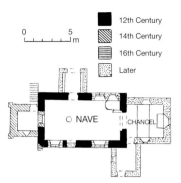

0   5 m

■ 12th Century
▨ 14th Century
▤ 16th Century
▦ Later

○ NAVE   CHANCEL

Plan of Syde Church

Tarlton Church

SUDELEY   *St Mary*   SO 032277

The embattled church was built c1460 by Ralph Boteler and lies in the grounds of the castle he had begun in the 1440s. It is five bays long with gargoyles and pinnacled buttresses between renewed windows with headstops to their hoodmoulds, and diagonal buttresses at the corners. Headstops on the west doorway are thought to represent Henry VI and Queen Margaret of Anjou. A chapel flanks the eastern three bays on the north side and there was once another small chapel by the second bay from the east on the south side, where a low-side window with 17th century Swiss glass looks in towards the altar. There may also have been been an east vestry. The interior was damaged during the conflicts of the 1640s and was restored with new furnishings in 1859-63, when a monument was erected to Henry VIII's sixth and last wife, Catherine Parr, d1548. There is much stained glass of the 1860s but windows in the north chapel have 13th, 14th and 16th century figures brought in from elsewhere. See page 132.

SYDE   *St Mary*   SO 949109

The chancel was rebuilt c1850 but there is a simple round-arched chancel arch and the nave has two early doorways, that on the south, now blocked, with a huge lintel that could be 10th or 11th century. A 15th century door with an iron closing ring remains in the north doorway, where the round arch has been filled in. The tie-beam and crown-post roof could be 13th century. There are 16th century windows in Norman embrasures. The tower arch of the small 14th century saddle-back roofed west tower is blocked and the ringing chamber is only reached from outside. On the north side is a 14th century window with an image niche. The late medieval octagonal font has quatrefoil panels with roses and a moulded base with gabled buttresses. The pulpit and box-pews are 18th century and the very decayed royal arms appear to be of Clarles II. One south window contains a roundel of 15th century glass showing St James of Compostella. There is a 13th century cross-slab near the porch.

TARLTON   *St Osmund*   ST 958999

In 1875 the church was remodelled with neo-Norman features after use as a farm building. Ancient features are the Norman chancel arch with chevrons and billets, the 15th century west window, and a font brought in from Rodmarton which is a Norman tub recut with low relief quatrefoils in the early 14th century.

TAYNTON   *St Lawrence*   SP 737221

This church was erected in the 1650s by Thomas Pury after the medieval church nearly a mile to the NE was wrecked during fighting in 1643. It is a single chamber set north to south, with doorways on either side near the north end. The north porch was added in 1825, the bellcote and windows date from 1864-5, and a large chancel was added in 1893-4. The font of c1660 with cherub's heads and acanthus leaves is set on a fluted stem. The Jacobean pulpit is from the church of Holy Trinity at Gloucester demolished in 1648. The internal north doorway appears to use parts from a 17th or 18th century reredos. There are tablets to John Holder, d1734, and Elizabeth Holder, d1765.

TEDDINGTON   *St Nicholas*   SO 964330

The chancel arch is Early Norman. Of c1200-20 is the north doorway with a pointed arch with a roll-moulding and a hoodmould with human and beast's head stops. The porch is probably 14th century, and the chancel is also of that date, the east window having reticulated tracery. The south windows of the nave are of 1627, one bearing that date, and around that time the side windows of the chancel lost their tracery. The diagonally buttressed west tower of 1567 has a fine late 13th century west window and a tower arch which are older material reused from Hailes Abbey. The window has a cusped circle over two light with cinquefoiled heads. Amongst other wall paintings in the nave are royal arms of William and Mary of 1689. The shaft of the font is 14th century work with ballflowers between the eight attached shafts. The pulpit is dated 1655 with the names of churchwardens. Other work of that period survives in the reading desk and altar rails. The 16th century benches have linenfold panelling.

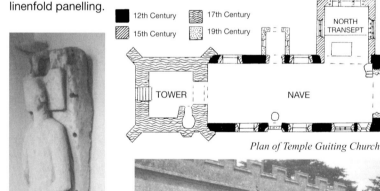

Plan of Temple Guiting Church

Effigy at Tetbury Church   *Temple Guiting Church*

Reset west window at Teddington

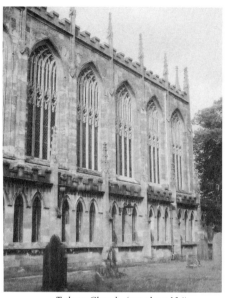

Tetbury Church (see also p134)

TEMPLE GUITING   St *Mary*   SP 091279

A Norman corbel-table survives on the chancel, and fragments of a Norman doorway have been reused in the north porch of 1884. An early 14th century lancet in the nave SE corner has a hoodmould with ballflowers and jester head-stops. The north transept was added in the early 16th century when the nave was given five new windows and parapets, plus a panelled roof. One window retains stained glass of saints, the other four now contain round-headed Classical style windows of the 1750s, when a Venetian window was inserted into the transept north wall. The large diagonally buttressed west tower with big pinnacles and gargoyles appears to be 17th century. The chancel was remodelled in 1884. The late 14th century octagonal font has pairs of four-leaved flowers. Furnishings of the 18th century include the pulpit, a reredos under the tower, royal arms of George II dated 1742 and a set of decayed hatchments. There are monuments to Reverend Dr George Talbot, d1785, repairer of the church, and John Beale, d1774.

TETBURY   St *Mary*   ST 890930

A minster church existed here by 681. The large medieval building was ruinous by the early 18th century and repairs of the 1740s were deemed inadequate. Except for a 14th century tower with a tall recessed spire the building was replaced by a new structure between 1777 and 1781. The existing tower is a facsimile rebuild of 1890-3. The church has a lofty nave and aisles of equal height, huge windows, and low passages set against the outer walls with arches through walls dividing seven bays. The tall clustered arcade columns are of wood and there are galleries on three sides. There are remains of two 14th century male effigies, and a fragment of a knight of c1300. There are also effigies dated 1586 of a couple of the Gastrell family. The wall tablets include those of Sir William Romney, d1611, Deborah Roche, d1720, Gilbert Gastrell, d1732, Joseph and Elizabeth Wickes, d1764, John Paul, d1787, Henry Harvey, d1789.

TEWKESBURY *St Mary*   SO 890324

The church of the Benedictine abbey founded by Robert FitzHamon c1087 has survived almost complete, having been purchased by the townsfolk when the monastery was dissolved in 1539. The townsfolk already had a right to worship in the nave, although that part was then for a while neglected in favour of services in the eastern part. The building was once 113m long but 20m of length was lost with the destruction of the Lady Chapel in the mid 16th century. The Norman church consecrated in 1121 probably replaced a Saxon minster and much of it still stands. It has an aisled nave 21m wide internally (including the aisles) and eight bays long, a north porch, a central tower with transepts, and an eastern arm with an apse with an ambulatory, off which probably projected three apsidal chapels, as at the similar abbey church at Gloucester. There were other apsidal chapels opening off the eastern sides of the transepts, that on the south still remaining with a vault with radiating ribs, whilst a 13th century chapel has replaced that on the north. The west front has a recessed arch with six orders of roll-mouldings and there are corner turrets with short spires, although proper towers over an extra ninth bay of each aisle were probably originally envisaged. The west window is a replacement of 1686 of a mid 14th century one destroyed in a gale in 1661.

The tall arcades of arches of two orders are carried on tall columns nearly two metres in diameter. Above is a low triforium. A new clerestory was provided in the 14th century, when a lierne vault was added. The centre bosses show the life of Christ and others have angels playing instruments. The aisles have oblong niches in the outer walls and also have 14th century windows and vaults. The north porch has a tunnel vault and the inner entrance has a composite lintel of joggled stones. Originally the eastern two bays of the nave were closed off by a pulpitum and screen, east of which lay the monastic choir. Outside the south aisle are traces of the former cloister, which had been rebuilt in the 15th century in imitation of that at Gloucester Abbey.

Tewkesbury Abbey Church

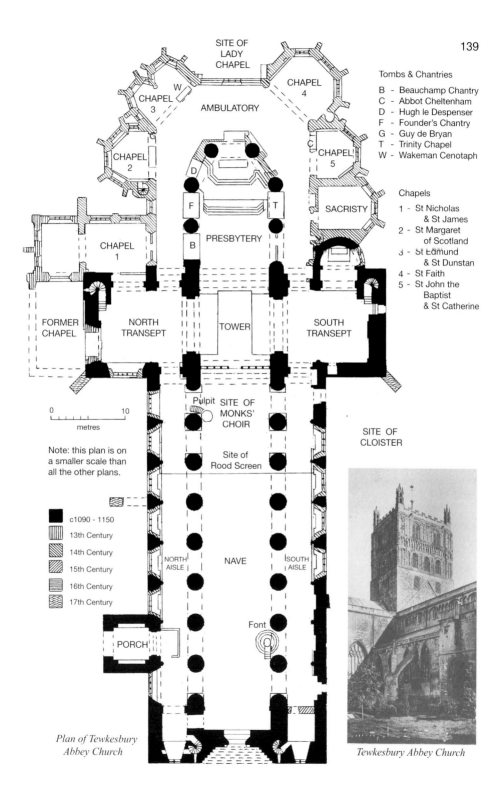

Tombs & Chantries

B - Beauchamp Chantry
C - Abbot Cheltenham
D - Hugh le Despenser
F - Founder's Chantry
G - Guy de Bryan
T - Trinity Chapel
W - Wakeman Cenotaph

Chapels

1 - St Nicholas
    & St James
2 - St Margaret
    of Scotland
3 - St Edmund
    & St Dunstan
4 - St Faith
5 - St John the
    Baptist
    & St Catherine

SITE OF LADY CHAPEL

CHAPEL 4

W

CHAPEL 3

AMBULATORY

CHAPEL 2

G

CHAPEL 5

SACRISTY

D

CHAPEL 1

F

T

PRESBYTERY

B

FORMER CHAPEL

NORTH TRANSEPT

TOWER

SOUTH TRANSEPT

Pulpit

SITE OF MONKS' CHOIR

SITE OF CLOISTER

Site of Rood Screen

Note: this plan is on a smaller scale than all the other plans.

0 ____ 10
metres

■ c1090 - 1150
▦ 13th Century
▨ 14th Century
▧ 15th Century
▤ 16th Century
▨ 17th Century

NORTH AISLE

NAVE

SOUTH AISLE

Font

PORCH

Plan of Tewkesbury Abbey Church

Tewkesbury Abbey Church

Chantry chapels in the east end of Tewkesbury Abbey Church

The central tower is the largest and finest of its period in England. The upper parts are mid 12th century, repaired in the 1930s, and have much arcading, chevrons, shafts with cushion capitals, and pairs of bell-openings. The bells, however, were hung in a detached 15th century tower to the NE, later used as the town gaol, but dismantled in 1816. There are battlements and pinnacles of 1660. The original wooden spire had fallen in 1559. Internally the tower has a lierne-vaut of the late 14th century. The transepts have two levels of arches below a low triforium and a clerestory which was later rebuilt. Each transept has a staircase in the eastern corner away from the central tower. To the north of the north transept lay a 13th century chapel of St Nicholas composed of a nave which has gone and chancel which still remains, with original aracading and later vaulting with the arms of the de Clares and Despencers.

The eastern arm of the church retains its six sturdy Norman circular piers, upon which are 14th century arches and a tall clerestory and a fine vault supported by flying buttresses. The clerestory windows contain stained glass of the 1340s with a scene of the Last Judgement in the east window and a Coronation of the Virgin in the rose. The western window glass depicts knights in surcoats with the arms of the FitzRoy, de Clare, Despenser, FitzHamon, and Zouch familes. Arms also appear of the Fitzalans and de Warennes. The eastern part of the ambulatory was widened and made polygonal in the 14th century rebuilding. The Lady Chapel extending east has gone but the other polygonal ended chapels still remain. The largest is that of St Faith facing SE, west of which is that of St Catherine, and then the sacristy, which has some old glass and ballflowers around the doorway. The NE chapel is arranged with double polygonal bays, allowing separate altars to St Edmund and St Dunstan. West of it is the chapel of St Margaret of Scotland. Below the Lady Chapel archway is an entrance to the vault where George, Duke of Clarence was buried after being drowned in a butt of Malmsey wine in 1477 after plotting against his brother Edward IV.

Tewkesbury Abbey Church contains many monuments and memorials and only a few of the oldest and most notable can be mentioned here. There are three stone-cage type chantry chapels set under the arcade arches close to the high altar. The earliest is that containing the kneeling effigy of Edward Dispenser, built in the five years after his death in 1375. The chantry of the founder Robert FitzHamon, d1107 built in the 1390s on the north side is similar. Even more splendid is that of Richard Beauchamp, Earl of Worcester, d1421 in the next bay to the west. The west end of this chantry has a fan-vaulted lower level and an upper level of uncertain purpose with a lierne vault. To the east is a tomb with effigies of Hugh, Lord Despencer, d1348 and his wife Elizabeth Montacute. On the other side of a ambulatory, at the entrance to St Margaret's Chapel, is the tomb of Guy de Brien, d1390, who was Elizabeth Montacute's second husband. A tomb at the entrance of the next chapel has an effigy of a body in a shroud and is associated with Abbot John Wakemen, d1549, although it is actually somewhat earlier By St Catherine's Chapel is the tomb of Abbot Cheltenham, d1509. Behind the sedilia is the burial place of Edward II's unpopular favourite Hugh Despenser, hanged by rebel lords in 1325, but the tombs here are of Abbot John Cotes, d1347, and Abbot Robert Forthington, d1254. There is also a tomb of Abbot Alan, d1202.

Other monuments around the church include a military effigy of c1350 in the north aisle, a 14th century tomb in the south aisle, a half effigy of John Roberts, d1631 in the north transept, a tablet to Joseph Reeve, d1651, a Classical tablet to Dr George Peyton, d1742, and a tablet of 1749 to the Mann family.

There are a few stalls with miserichords and the font has a stem of c1320 with ballflowers, although the base may be earlier and the bowl is 19th century. There are old screens, royal arms of Queen Anne, and an organ of c1580 with embossed tin pipes and a contemporary case which has come from Magdalen College, Oxford.

The east end of Tewkesbury Abbey Church   *West front at Tewkesbury*

Tibberton Church

Herringbone masonry at Tibberton Church

Todenham Church

TIBBERTON   *Holy Trinity*   SO 737221

Herringbone masonry on both sides of the nave and on the north side of the chancel suggests an 11th century date. In the south wall are a blocked doorway and traces of two early windows, and there is a simple round chancel arch. The chancel was lengthened in the 13th century and has two lancets of that date, but the east triplet is of 1908. Several windows and the tower with a NE staircase turret are 14th century.

TIRLEY   *St Michael*   SO 840285

The lowest stage of the diagonally buttressed tower may be late 13th century, although it has a 14th century west window with reticulated tracery and a 15th century top. The nave has 14th and 15th century windows on the south side and 19th century ones on the north. There is a much restored timber-framed south porch of c1500. The chancel has 15th century windows, but the east window is probably of 1894. The altar rails and altar table are 17th century and there is a late medieval chest. The tub font may be Norman. Over the chancel arch are faint royal arms of the 18th century. There are monuments to Anne Turton, d1642, William Hurdman, d1684, Mary Browne, d1717, Robert Gittos, d1724, and Thomas Hopkins, d1789.

TODDINGTON   *St Andrew*   SP 035331

This is an impressive estate church of 1868-9 designed by G.E.Street. Earlier relics are the 18th century chalice-shaped font, fragments of effigies of a 16th century female and a 17th century man, and tablets to Charles Tracy, d1676, Viscount Tracy, d1756, who partly rebuilt the previous church in 1723, and Viscount Tracy, d1792.

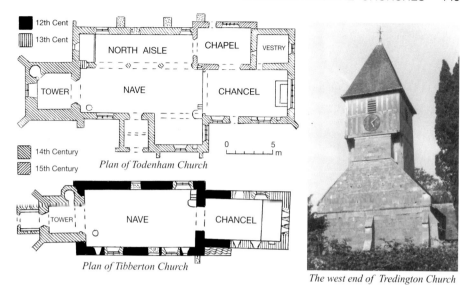

Plan of Todenham Church

Plan of Tibberton Church

The west end of Tredington Church

TODENHAM   *St Thomas Becket*   SP 244364

The nave, chancel, NE vestry and south transept are all early 14th century work and the only older relics are the Norman east respond of the north arcade and part of a double-chamfered arch at the west end. There are continuous stringcourses inside and out and a fine east window with restored flowing tracery. In a second, slightly later campaign the aisle was rebuilt with a new three-bay arcade, and the south porch and ashlar-faced west tower and broach spire added. The spire has pinnacles at the angles and two-light lucarnes with crocketed ogival heads on each of the eight sides. It was rebuilt in 1772 after being damaged by a storm. The porch has a roof of stone slabs supported on a stone arch. The chancel has a trefoil-headed piscina and three sedilia with crocketed ogival heads. The priest's doorway has an external finial and an ogival head. Several new windows were inserted c1500, along with a roodloft staircase, and the north chapel of the Holy Trinity was built from a bequest of 1513 from the will of William Grevil. In 1773 the churchwardens had their names inscribed on the 13th century font set on a 15th century stem. A brass has figures of William Molton, d1604, and his wife. On the outside of the chancel is a tablet to John Mander, d1723.

TREDINGTON   *St John the Baptist*   SO 905296

The Norman nave has over the north doorway a weathered tympanum with Christ and two kneeling figures holding books. The south doorway has two orders of chevrons and voussoirs of alternating limestone and sandstone. The hoodmould has pellets and a dragon-headstop. One shaft has twisted ornamentation and the other chevrons. The low chancel arch of two orders has a hoodmould with foliage and chamfered imposts. Above it is a rood beam. The chancel was lengthened in the 13th or 14th century and there are several 14th and 15th century windows, one on the north side having some fragments of medieval glass, whilst the south porch is dated 1624. The fine coved plaster ceiling of the nave is probably 17th century. At the west end are braced timbers supporting the belfry. There are old benches and Jacobean altar-rails. Outside is a 14th century churchyard cross with a 20th century top.

Hancock monument at Twyning

Tirley Church

TURKDEAN   *All Saints*   SP 108175

A small 15th century tower was built within the west end of the Norman nave, where there survive pilaster buttresses, fragments of the corbel-tables, and traces of the former Norman north and south doorways. Further east the nave was rebuilt in the 15th century, when a north porch was added. There are head-stops on the outer entrance of the porch. The south aisle with a three bay arcade is late 14th century and there is part of a wall-painting of that period on one of the spandrels. There is a stone 15th century pulpit. Over the chancel arch are very worn royal arms.

Turkdean Church

TWYNING   *St Mary Magdalene*   SO 894360

The bellframe in the diagonally buttressed west tower has been dated to c1452-3 by dendrochronology. The long and wide nave has Early Norman pilaster buttresses and one blocked original north window and the heads of two others. The north doorway has shafts with cushion capitals, a roll-moulded arch and a plain tympanum. On either side are pilaster strips with niches. The chancel arch is 14th century upon Norman imposts. The neo-Norman windows are of 1867-70, when the chancel was rebuilt. An organ chamber was added in 1886, and a vestry in 1897. There is a plain 15th century octagonal font. In the chancel is a monument with an effigy of Sybil Clare, d1575, and there are tablets to Edwin Baldwyn, d1669, and Captain George Maxwell, d1779. In the tower is a monument with half-effigies of William Hancock, d1676 and his sons.

ULEY   *St Giles*   ST 791985

The church was entirely rebuilt in 1857-8 and the only older relics are an octagonal font of c1200 with pairs of shallow arches on each face and several tablets high up in the tower including those of Edward Dorney, d1700, John Eyles, 1731, and the Reverend Thomas Gregory, d1778.

UPLEADON   *St Mary*   SO 769270

The church lies on a rather unstable clay mound and has only a farm for company. The Norman nave retains original windows on both sides above a billet stringcourse. The north doorway has chevrons, beaded cable moulding, capitals on the shafts with a scallop and animal heads, and a tympanum showing the Agnus Dei within a cabled roundel flanked by lions. The chancel was rebuilt in 1847-9, when a south porch was added. The north vestry is of 1884. There is a timber-framed west tower of c1500 with cross-bracing only visible inside. The nave has a kingpost truss roof of the 16th or 17th century. The pulpit is dated 1661.

Twyning Church

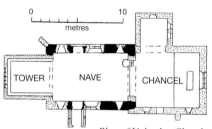

Plan of Upleadon Church

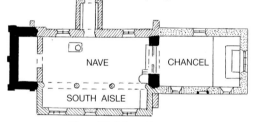

Plan of Turkdean Church

Norman doorway at Upleadon Church

Interior of Upleadon Church

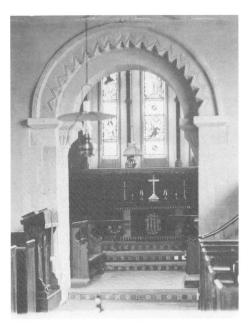

Chancel arch at Upper Swell

Upper Slaughter Church

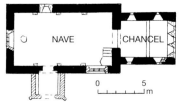

Plan of Upper Swell Church

UPPER SLAUGHTER   *St Peter*   SP 155232

In the early 15th century a tower was built within the west end of the Late Norman nave. What was originally a pointed chancel arch of c1200 of three orders with chevrons and crenellations now forms a tower arch, and the tower vault lies on Norman beakheads. The 14th century chancel has a cinquefoiled piscina, separate ogee-headed sedilia and a three light east window with intersecting tracery. A mortuary chapel was added on the north side in 1854. In the restoration of 1876-7 the nave south wall was rebuilt and a south porch added in which are loose stones from the Norman south doorway. The Late Norman north arcade was rebuilt, using some old parts, and the aisle (which has been widened in 1822) was extended. There is a fine octagonal font of c1400 with ogival panels. In the Easter Sepulchre recess in the chancel is a Baroque tomb to Frances and Andrew Wanley, d1688. There are also brass plates to John Slaughter, d1583, and his wife and son, d1597, and a tablet to Joseph Stone, d1681.

UPPER SWELL   *St Mary*   SP 177269

There are four Norman windows in the chancel and the chancel arch has two orders with chevrons, and there are also chevrons on the south doorway, which has one order of shafts with volute capitals. The chancel SE window also forms a sedile and has in its east jamb a 14th century ogival-headed piscina. The east window is of 1872. The nave has an old trussed rafter roof and a south window of c1500 with a pedestal for a statue. There is also a restored 13th century window. There is a tiny rib-vault over a niche over the outer entrance of the 15th century porch. The octagonal 15th century font has quatrefoils, flowers, a shield and an angel and there are panels on the stem. There is a monument to the Reverend Henry Brownam, d1795.

Upton St Leonards Church   *Norman doorway at Upton St Leonards*

UPTON ST LEONARDS   *St Leonard*   SP 862150

The diagonally buttressed west tower is 14th century but has a reset Norman door-way. The south aisle is of 1835, and the north aisle and and porch were mostly rebuilt in 1845-6. The 14th century north chapel was restored in 1849-50, when the chancel was rebuilt. A south chapel and vestry were added in 1889. The north arcade appears to have one pier of c1200. There is Norman tub-font. There is a large monument to Sir Thomas Snell, d1754 in the north chapel. Two chest tombs of c1650 lie by the porch.

WESTCOTE   *St Mary*   SP 220205

The chancel was rebuilt in 1875-6, when a north vestry was added, and the nave was mostly rebuilt in 1886, when a south porch was added. On the north side are a blocked 15th century doorway, a head of c1400 with a cleft beard, and renewed 14th and 15th century windows. The tower arch is 15th century but the tower itself was rebuilt in 1901-2. There is a 15th century font. The octagonal base of a churchyard cross of c1300 with worn figures in trefoil-headed niches was brought here from Gawcombe.

WESTONBIRT   *St Catherine*   ST 864895

The church lies away from the village and now serves as the chapel of the school in the adjoining house. It has a south transeptal tower with a 15th century top with gargoyles on a 14th century diagonally buttressed base containing a former chapel with a squint to the chancel. The south porch with a trefoil-headed stoup is also 14th century. The 13th century double piscina and the 14th century east window with flowing tracery were reset in 1840 when the chancel was rebuilt and a north aisle added. The chancel arch and the west wall were rebuilt in 1878. In 1955 the chancel was given a north aisle and a south vestry. The octagonal 15th century font has quatrefoils and a panelled stem. The only pre-Victorian monument is a tablet to Betty Tugwell, d1768. See p148.

Westonbirt Church

Weston-sub-Edge Church

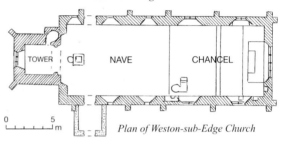

0   5
⌊___⌋ m

Plan of Weston-sub-Edge Church

WESTON SUB EDGE   *St Lawrence*   SP 128407

The wide 14th century nave and chancel are undivided and have internal and external stringcourses. The nave has trefoil-headed north and south doorways and trefoil-headed lancets and the chancel has windows with restored geometrical tracery and a trefoil-headed piscina and two aumbries. The west tower is 15th century. The font has a 13th century base. The pulpit is Jacobean and there are royal arms of Queen Anne. Beneath nodding ogee-headed canopies are two small 14th century effigies. There is a brass of William Hodges, d1590, and a tablet to Pharamus Fiennes, d1708.

Whaddon Church

WHADDON

St Margaret SO 833137

The lancets of the 13th century nave and chancel appear to have been widened. The moulded north doorway has headstops. The 15th century tower has gargoyles and buttresses which are diagonal below and clasping above. Also of that period is the octagonal font with three trefoil-headed niches on each side and a panelled stem. There are royal arms of George III. The furnishings are mostly of the time of the restoration of 1854.

WHITMINSTER

St Andrew SO 760091

The 14th century south doorway has a door with good original ironwork.The tall tower of c1500 with a higher NE staircase turret bears the dates 1763 and 1844, when it was repaired. Also of c1500 are the south porch and the unrestored parts of the chancel. The priest's doorway has foliage spandrels and the letters PB probably referring to the priory of Bruton in Somerset, which held the church. In the restoration of 1884-5 the original east window was reset in a new vestry which forms an extension of a north aisle added in 1841-2. The pulpit is Jacobean. Beneath the altar is part of a 13th century cross-slab. There are kneeling figures of Rebecca Lloyd, d1625 and three children, and nearby is a tablet to her husband Thomas, d1658. There is also a tablet to John Bray, d1797.

Whitminster Church

WHITTINGTON   *St Bartholomew* SP 014206

Two separate arches, one Norman and the other 15th century with good headstops of a man in a cap and a lady with a horned head-dress, open into a narrow and short south aisle with a part of a blocked Norman window in its west wall. Reset in the 19th vestry are part of a Norman arch with chevrons and roll-mouldings and the head of a 13th century lancet. East of the aisle is a late 16th century chapel with two original windows and a two bay arcade of 1872. The chancel has a 14th century east window. The nave has a blocked 16th century west doorway with foliage spandrels. The font is 13th century. There is a 14th century tomb recess in the nave. In the chapel are 14th century effigies of a lady with a wimple and two knights with long surcoats, all members of the Crupes family. There are brasses of Richard Coton, d1556, and his wife Margaret. The best of several 17th and 18th century tablets is that of Thomas Tracy, d1770. To the east of the church lies a 14th century churchyard cross with a tall shaft.

Effigy at Whittington

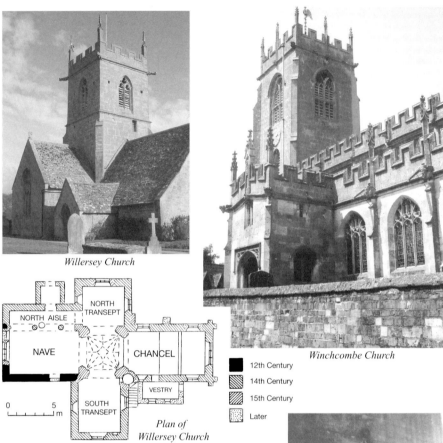

Willersey Church

Winchcombe Church

Plan of Willersey Church

■	12th Century
▨	14th Century
▧	15th Century
▢	Later

WILLERSEY   *St Peter*   SP 107397

The blocked south doorway is Norman. The narrow
north aisle rebuilt in the 14th century had a three bay
arcade with octagonal piers but the eastern arch was
truncated when a central tower on finely moulded
arches of five orders was inserted c1400-20. The
lierne vault under the tower dates from the restoration of 1866-72, but the angels carrying shields are
15th century work. The transepts have 14th century
windows and there is an ogee-headed piscina in the
south transept, but the north transept has a large
15th century north window. The 14th century chancel has been heavily restored and the priest's doorway now leads to a vestry. There is a Norman tub
font. There are fragments of old glass in the tracery
of the fine 15th century west window. The earliest of
serveral tablets is that of John Scott, d1788.

Monument at Winchcombe

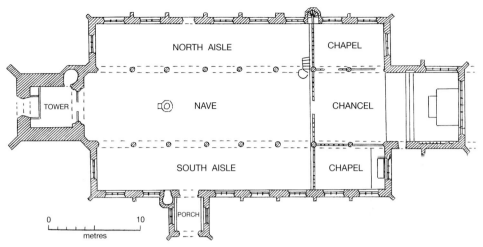

Plan of Winchcombe Church

WINCHCOMBE   *St Peter*   SP 023283

The entire building dates from the 1460s, the chancel being paid for by the former Benedictine abbey immediately to the north then under the abbacy of William Winchcombe, and the nave paid for by local wool merchants and Sir Ralph Boteler of nearby Sudeley Castle. His arms and those of the abbey appear on a stone tabernacle over the piscina. The nave, aisles and two storey south porch all have parapets with pinnacles and a fine series of grotesque heads. The porch has a concave-moulded architrave with quatrefoils in the spandrels and an angel supporting an image niche. A NW turret staircase leads to an upper room over a lierne-vault. The diagonally buttressed west tower has two-light windows in the second stage and four-light windows in the top stage, and there are gargoyles and pinnacles on the embattled parapet. There are arcades of eight bays with four-centred arches with concave mouldings set upon octagonal piers. The eastern two arches open into chapels flanking the western half of the chancel. Screens formed the only subdivisions. The original chapel screens remain in situ but the chancel screen was moved to a new location in front of the tower arch in 1984. Over the arcades are clerestory windows of four lights. The triple sedilia separated by image niches with brackets and crocketed canopies may be earlier work of c1400 reset. It appears that a vestry beyond the east wall existed or was planned.

The octagonal pedestal of the font is dated 1634, whilst the bowl is of later in the 17th century. The 18th century chest incorporates an early medieval dug-out chest. The almsbox is probably late 16th century. An early 16th century altar cloth with the pomegranite badge of Catherine of Aragon has been made up from priests' copes of the 1380s. The chandelier is of 1753, there are royal arms of George III of 1778, and there is an organ case of c1735. In the north aisle are two cases of medieval tiles from the abbey site and a carved door with the initials of Richard Kidderminster, abbot from 1488 to 1525. Also from the abbey are the pair of large stone 13th century coffins. Several windows have minor fragments of medieval stained glass. There is a kneeling effigy of Thomas Williams, d1636. There are tablets to William and Collis Smart, d1772, and Ann Trotman, d1787 and several more of the early 19th century.

Head at Winchcombe

Tomb in the churchyard at Windrush

WINDRUSH *St Peter* SO 194130

The Norman south doorway has two complete orders of beakheads with almond-shaped eyes. The shafts have scalloped capitals and palmettes on the abaci. On the hoodmould is a sawtooth motif. The ornate jambs of the chancel arch lean outwards. A twist motif appears on the south and lozenges and beaded chevrons on the north. The double-chamfered pointed arch is slightly later. The early 13th century three bay south arcade has octagonal capitals on circular piers with roll-moulded bases. A blocked round-headed lancet remains in the west end of the aisle. The aisle south wall and the nave north wall were given plain parapets and square-headed windows in the 15th century. The 14th century south transept has a south window with reticulated tracery and a cinquefoil-headed piscina. The 15th century west tower has a SE staircase turret and a double-hollow-chamfered tower arch. The chancel has a 14th century trussed rafter roof but was otherwise mostly rebuilt in 1873-4, when the south vestry and organ chamber were added. The octagonal font with quatrefoils and trefoil-headed panels on the stem is 15th century. The pulpit is Jacobean. There are 18th century ledger stones to the Broad family in the nave, and a stone to George Hungerford, d1597. See p6.

WINSON *St Michael* SO 091086

This small Early Norman church was a chapel-of-ease to Bibury. On the north side is a pilaster buttress and a blocked doorway with a round arch with a billeted hoodmould and shafts with scalloped capitals, and a window remains in the chancel. There is a similar doorway on the south side. In the 13th century the chancel was heightened and given a new east wall with a lancet under a hoodmould. There are low-side windows on either side, that on the south below a lancet. The chancel roof may also be partly 13th century. Another lancet remains to the west of the 15th century south porch in which is an ogival-headed niche on the east side. The west wall was mostly rebuilt in the 1880s. A Norman font is set upon four 19th century shafts. The semi-octagonal stone pulpit with traceried panels has either been scraped or is a facsimile copy of medieval original. There is a group of 18th century chest tombs by the porch.

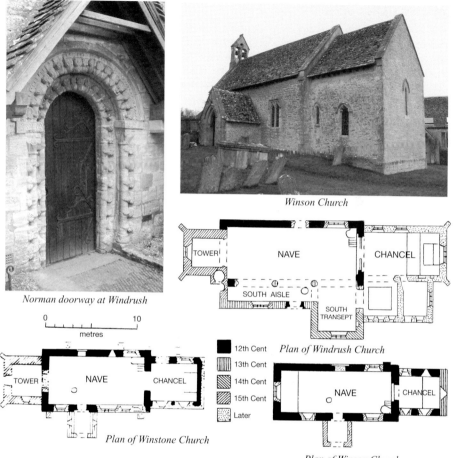

Norman doorway at Windrush

Winson Church

0   10
metres

TOWER   NAVE   CHANCEL

SOUTH AISLE

SOUTH TRANSEPT

■ 12th Cent   *Plan of Windrush Church*
▦ 13th Cent
▨ 14th Cent
▧ 15th Cent
▦ Later

TOWER   NAVE   CHANCEL

Plan of Winstone Church

NAVE   CHANCEL

Plan of Winson Church

WINSTONE   *St Bartholomew*   SO 966094

The nave and chancel are probably both late 11th century and there is no east window. The blocked north doorway has monolithic jambs of Saxon type and a huge flat lintel with a chamfered upper edge. Above is a round arch surmounted by a head. An adjacent window has been cut from a single slab. The south doorway has jambs of through stones. The shafts have bulbous bases and scalloped capitals and there is a diaper pattern on the lintel. There is a roll around the tympanum with an inciseed lozenge pattern. The foot of each jamb has been cut away, supposedly to allow the largest bell to enter the church. The north jamb of the chancel arch is formed from a single stone, whilst the south jamb is formed of four through-stones. The chancel was mostly rebuilt in 1875-6, when a north vestry was added and the nave given buttresses. Several single and paired trefoil-headed lancets were inserted in the late 13th century when the porch was added, and there is a four-light south window probably of the 1570s. The doorway into the saddleback-roofed 15th century west tower is now blocked. There is an octagonal 15th century font. Seven early grave markers with splay-armed crosses are built into the chancel walls. There is a tablet to John Haviland, d1638.

WITHINGTON   *St Michael*   SP 031157

There was a minster here in the 7th century. The manor subsequently belonged to the bishops of Worcester. By the end of the 12th century the church had a nave, central tower and a small chancel. There is a renewed Norman window on the north side of the tower, and a Norman corbel-table lies on the chancel, possibly reset during a 13th century lengthening. There are chevrons on the north and south doorways, the latter also having flowers, a hoodmould with daisies with beast-headstops, and two orders of shafts with scalloped capitals. The nave has traces of several 13th century lancets, including a group of three in the west wall and by c1300 a south porch and a second stage to the tower had been added. The south transept with a fine south window is 14th century. Under the tower the east and south arches are 13th or 14th century and the west arch is rebuilt Norman work. In the 15th century a clerestory was added to the nave and a tall top stage to the tower with large four-light bell-openings with ogival-arched crocketed hoodmoulds, and gargoyles and pinnacles. Also of that period are a lower window in the nave for an altar with a piscina, and another in the chancel. In the chancel north wall is a trefoil-headed niche which seems to have contained a water cistern. The nave contains a restored 14th cetury tomb recess with ballflowers and a crocketed canopy. In the chancel are a weathered effigy of a priest of c1400, and a brass inscription to Sybil Knollis, d1614. High up in the nave SW corner are effigies of Sir John Howe, d1670 and his wife Bridget, moved here from the transept. Other tablets include those of Gilbert Osborne, d1656, and John Eycott, d1789.

WOODCHESTER

St Mary   SO 839032

The medieval church was abandoned after completion in 1864 of a new church a third of a mile to the south, to which were taken the tomb chest with effigies of Sir George Huntley, d1622 and his wife, plus tablets to Nathaniel Peach, d1719, Robert Bridges, d1722, James Smith, d1757, and Edward Peach, d1770. Two walls remain of the old church with a Norman north doorway with two orders of shafts, a Norman chancel arch with shafts and two orders of roll-mouldings, and one 15th century window.

Withington Church

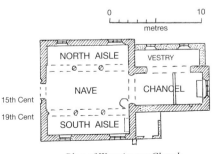

Plan of Wormington Church

Saxon crucifix at Wormington

Head on arch respond
at Yanworth

Woodchester Old Church

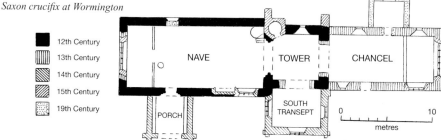

Plan of Withington Church

WOOLSTONE *St Martin* SO 961303

The 14th century chancel has an effigy of a priest of that period and a large image niche with pinnacles and a canopy beside the east window with reticulated tracery and a hoodmould with headstops. Three blocked arches of an arcade to a former north aisle of c1500 are visible in the north wall. The south windows of the chancel are also of that period. The 15th century west tower with pinnacles and gargoyles has developed a lean because the clay subsoil here is unable to properly carry its weight. The south porch was added in 1877 and the north vestry is of 1975. The octagonal font with a rectangular moulded panel on each face is late 14th century. There is a ledger stone to John Roberts, d1650, and a monument to Elizabeth Bishop, d1765.

WORMINGTON *St Catherine* SP 039364

There are Norman corbels reset below the weatherboarded and castellated bell-turret probably added c1800, when the west wall was rebuilt. A two bay 19th century north chapel now forms a vestry. The nave and aisles with three bay arcades and the narrow chancel are the product of a rebuilding in the 1470s at the expense of Hailes Abbey, and also of that period is the octagonal font with quatrefoils and niches on five sides of the pedestal. The aisle east ends form mini transepts. There are fragments of old glass in the western windows of the aisles. The incised slab of a man with two wives may be of John Daston, d1532. On the south aisle east wall is a Crucifixion of c1020-50 found at Wormington Grange. The composition also features the Hand of God.

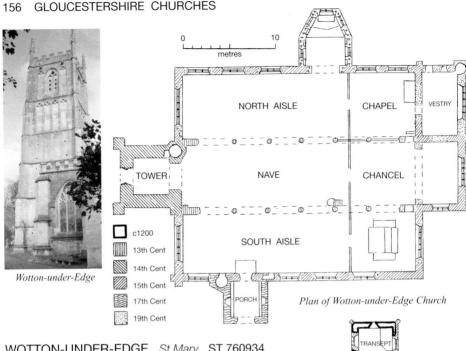

Wotton-under-Edge

Plan of Wotton-under-Edge Church

c1200

13th Cent

14th Cent

15th Cent

17th Cent

19th Cent

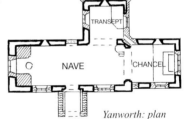

Yanworth: plan

WOTTON-UNDER-EDGE   *St Mary*   ST 760934

The lower stages of the west tower are of c1330 there being ballflowers on the west doorway. The upper stages with a panelled parapet with crocketed pinnacles is of c1370. The wide aisles are 15th century, but the parapets and window tracery have been renewed. Unrestored windows remain in the chancel. The two storey south porch was rebuilt in 1658. There are pinnacled ogival-headed niches on either side of the upper window. Inside are 13th century arcades of six bays, although the two eastern bays on each side are of 1838. The north side has round piers with foliage capitals and the south side has alternating round and octagonal piers. A consecration here is recorded in 1283. A clerestory was added in the 15th century. When the roof was raised in the 18th century the clerestory was rebuilt, the original window heads probably being reset upon taller new mullions. Plaster ceilings were inserted in 1800 and 1805. The chapel on the north side of the north aisle was rebuilt in 1780 to form a polygonal-ended vestry with a fireplace. The organ was acquired in 1799 from the church of St Martin-in-the-Fields, Westminster, to whom it had been given by George I in 1726. On a a a tomb chest are large and fine brasses of Thomas, Lord Berkeley, d1417 and his wife Margaret. She has a dog with collar and bells, and he, being an admiral, has a mermaid collar. Only the indent remains of a cross-brass to the priest Richard de Wotton, d1329. The many wall monuments include those of Robert Webb c1660, the Dawes brothers, d1712, Thomas Rous, d1737, John Nelmes, d1742, Richard Osborne, d1749, Daniel Adey, d1752, Mary Blagden, d1761, Anne Moore, d1765, William Adey, d1765, John Osborne, d1770, the Reverend William Taswell, d1775, William Veel, d1783, and Robert Veel, d1787. See picture on page 10.

WYCK RISSINGTON   *St Laurence*   SP 192215

The late 13th century chancel has a unique east end with two pairs of tall lancets each surmountedv by a concave-sided lozenge-shaped light, with a third such light near the apex of the gable. Stringcourses rising around these features tie the design together. The north wall has three lancets and another remains on the south, along with one window from each of the 14th and 15th centuries and a shouldered-lintelled priest's doorway. The massively walled west tower with lancets, angle buttresses and a sharply pointed tower arch of three chamfered orders is also 13th century. In the nave south wall is a blocked 13th century arch for a former south transept removed in 1879, when a short north aisle was added with a porch west of it. The plain Norman north doorway was reset to connect the aisle and porch. Also Norman are the lengths of corbel tables on the nave walls. There is tub-font of c1200 on a 19th century base. A Jacobean altar table stands on a medieval altar slab which was reused as a memorial slab in the late 16th century. There are twelve carved 16th century Flemish wooden roundels in the chancel. They depict the Joyful, Sorrowful and Glorious Mysteries of the Gospels. The lancets contain fragments of 14th cetury stained glass. In the porch are fragments of a 13th century cross-slab.

YANWORTH   *St Michael*   SP 079139

This ashlar-faced church of c1200 lies amongst the barns of a farm some way from the village. An original moulded plinth is carried round the nave, chancel and north transept, and all three parts retain one Norman window, whilst the nave also has a blocked north doorway and a south doorway with chevrons, keeled jambs with foliage capitals and a roll-moulding. The pointed chancel arch has a billeted hoodmould. In the 15th century the transept was given new east and west windows and a squint to the chancel, whilst the nave was given a new west window, parapets, and a tiny tower set upon blocks of masonry inserted in the western corners. The chancel also has a 15th century window. The south porch and the plain windows on either side of it are probably 17th century. There is a Norman tub font. On either side of the tower arch are wall paintings showing Death as a skeleton holding a dart, shroud and spade. There are metal tablets on the outside of the chancel to Thomas Bicknell, d1750 and his wife.

Chancel at Wyck Rissington

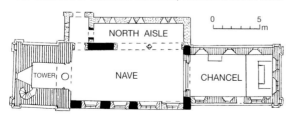

Wyck Rissington Church

Yanworth Church

OTHER ANGLICAN CHURCHES IN GLOUCESTERSHIRE

Not included in this list are churches in South Gloucestershire and the Forest of Dean, nor any of the Victorian churches mentioned in the main gazetteer of the book.

AMBERLEY - Holy Trinity - Built in 1836 for David Ricardo. Church hall in crypt.
APPERLEY - Holy Trinity - 1856 and 1890 by Charles Penrose. Thin campanile.
ASTON MAGNA - St John - 1846. Nave & chancel, paired lancets, and west tower.
BENTHAM - St Peter - 1888 by Foster & Okeley. Cruciform with lancets. No tower.
BIRDLIP - St Mary - 1957 by H.Stratton Davis, replacing a burnt out church of 1897.
BOX - St Barnabas - 1953 by Peter Falconer.
BRIMSCOMBE - Holy Trinity - Built 1840 for David Ricardo in Romanesque style.
BUSSAGE - St Michael - 1846 by J.P.Harrison. Aisle & porch added 1854 by Bodley.
CAINSCROSS - St Matthew - 1835-7 by C.Baker. Chancel added 1898 by W.Plank.
CERNEY WICK - Holy Trinity - 1847. Nave and chancel in style of c1300.
CHARLTON KINGS - Holy Apostles - 1871 by John Middleton.
CHAXHILL - St Luke - 1894 by Medland & Son. Brick, with an east apse.
CHELTENHAM - All Saints - 1868 by John Middleton. Apsidal chancel. At Pittville.
CHELTENHAM - Christ Church - 1838-40 by R.W & C.Fearrad. Interior of 1888-93.
CHELTENHAM - Emmanuel - 1936 by H.Rainger. Neo-Georgian. No east window.
CHELTENHAM - Holy Trinity - 1820-3. George Allen Underwood. Central west tower.
CHELTENHAM - St Aidan - 1959 by W.L.Barrow. Visible concrete frame.
CHELTENHAM - St James - 1825 by Edward Jenkins. Wide, with embattled aisles.
CHELTENHAM - St Mark - 1862-7 by John Middleton. West tower with spire.
CHELTENHAM - St Matthew - 1878-9 by Ewan Christian. NW tower, no spire now.
CHELTENHAM - Michael - 1965-6 by D.Stratton-Davis. Hexagonal.
CHELTENHAM - St Paul - 1827-31 by John B.Forbes. Ionic front. Cupola tower top.
CHELTENHAM - St Peter - 1847-9 by S.Whitfield Daukes. Cruciform. Neo-Norman.
CHELTENHAM - St Stephen - 1890, chancel 1893, organ chamber & vestry 1896.
CIRENCESTER - Holy Trinity - 1850-1 by Sir George Gilbert Scott, NW tower & spire.
CLEEVE HILL - St Peter - 1907 by E.D.Hoyland. Roughcast. Nave, chancel and aisle.
CLIFFORD'S MESNE - St Peter - 1882 by E.S.Harris. Bellcote over chancel arch.
COALPIT HEATH - St Saviour - 1844 by William Butterfield. Early 14th century style.
EASTCOMBE - St Augustine - Small mission church of 1868 by Henry Woodyer.
EDGE - St John the Baptist - 1865 by S.W.Daukes. Rock-faced. Bell-turret on porch.
FRAMILODE - St Peter - 1854 by Francis Niblett. North porch-tower. Neo-Norman.
FRAMPTON MANSELL - St Luke - 1844 by J.Parish. Neo-Norman.Apse, south tower.
FRANCE LYNCH - St John the Baptist - 1855-7, first complete church by G.F.Bodley.
GLOUCESTER - All Saints - 1875 by Sir G.G.Scott. Aisled nave and a south chapel.
GLOUCESTER - Christ Church - 1822 by Rickman & Hutchinson. West end c1900.
GLOUCESTER - St Aldate - 1964 by Robert Potter & Richard Here. Fan-shaped.
GLOUCESTER - St Barnabas - 1939-40 by N.F.Cachemaille-Day. Concrete & brick.
GLOUCESTER - St James - 1837-41 by Sampson Kempthorne. Chancel added 1879
GLOUCESTER - St Mark - 1847 by Francis Niblett. Aisles with lancets. Tower & spire
GLOUCESTER - St Oswald - 1939 by Ellery Anderson. Brick Basilica. South tower.
GLOUCESTER - St Paul - 1882-3 by Capel N.Tripp. South tower left unfinished.
GLOUCESTER - St Stephen - 1895 by Walter Plank. West baptistry by H.A.Dancey
GORSLEY - Christ Church - 1892-3 by Rollinson. Shallow transepts. East apse.
HANHAM - Christ Church - 1842 by Thomas Foster. Chancel added 1897.
HIGHNAM - Holy Innocents - 1847-51 by Henry Woodyer. Large, fine, good frescoes.
HILLSLEY - St Giles - 1851 by Rev Benjamin Perkins. Aisles. Mostly lancet windows.

HUCCLECOTE - St Philip & St James - 1850 by John Jacques & Son. Aisle 1911.
LONGLEVENS - Holy Trinity - 1935 by H.Stratton-Davis. West porches. Narrow aisles
LOWER CAM - St Bartholomew - 1844 by the incumbent, George Madan.
NAILSWORTH - All Saints - 1866 by Clissold. Nave, chancel, porch and bellcote.
NAILSWORTH - St George - 1898-1900 by M.H.Medland. Porch-tower not complete.
OAKRIDGE - St Bartholomew - 1837 by Robert Stokes. Nave, chancel & West tower.
PAXFORD - 1866 - Nave and chancel with bellcote in middle. School attached.
POULTON - St Michael - 1873 by William Butterfield. Older work in south porch.
REDWICK - 1840. Neo-Norman. Tower has gabled parapet on arcade. Now closed.
SELSEY - All Saints - 1862 by G.F.Bodley. Notable Morris & Co stained glass.
SHEEPSCOMBE - St John - c1820. Picturesque tower. Enlarged 1072 by F.Niblett.
OLAD - Holy Trinity - 1831-4 by Charles Baker. Altered 1868-9 by B.Bucknall.
STROUD - All Saints - 1908-10 by Temple Moore. Unfinished. Aisles. No chancel.
STROUD - Holy Trinity - 1938 by Thomas Foster. Wide nave. Polygonal apse.
STROUD - St Alban - 1915-16. Small neo-Norman church with an east apse.
TETBURY - St Saviour - 1848 by 1848 by S.W.Daukes & Hamilton. 14th century style.
TEWKESBURY - Holy Trinity - 1837 by Ebenezer Trotman. Red brick with west arch.
TRESHAM - 1855 by J.J.Rowland. Neo-Norman nave & chancel, bellcote & porch.
TWIGWORTH - St Matthew - 1842-4 by T.Fulljames. Chancel & south aisle 1891.
UP HATHERLEY - St Philip & St James - 1885 by Prothero & Phillott. Older font.
WELFORD - St Anne - 1864 by G.E.Street. Apse with trefoil-headed lancets.
WHITESHILL -St Paul - 1839-41 by Thomas Foster. Neo-Norman. Tower & east apse.

FURTHER READING

Buildings of England: Gloucestershire 1: The Cotwolds, D.Verey & A.Brooks, 2000
Buildings of England: Gloucestershire 2: Vale & Forest of Dean, Verey & Brooks, 2002
Old Gloucestershire Churches, W.Hobart Bird, 1928
Parish Churches of The Forest of Dean, Mike Salter, 1991
The Monumental Brasses of Gloucestershire. Cecil Davis, 1899
Transactions of the Bristol and Gloucestershire Archaeological Society.
Victoria County History of Gloucestershire, several volumes. series not yet complete.
Pamphlet guides exist for all the major churches and many of the minor ones.

Sedilia at Northleach Church

Chalford Church

A GLOSSARY OF TERMS

Abacus	-	Flat slab on top of a capital on a column, pier or respond.
Apse	-	Semicircular or polygonal east end of a church or chapel containing an altar.
Ashlar	-	Masonry of blocks with even faces and square edges fitted closely together.
Baroque	-	A whimsical and odd form of the Classical architectural style.
Beakheads	-	Decorative bird or beast heads, often biting a roll-moulding. Used c1120-95.
Broaches	-	Sloping half-pyramids adapting an octagonal spire to a square tower.
Cartouche	-	A tablet with an ornate frame, usually enclosing an inscription.
Chancel	-	The eastern part of a church used by the clergy and choir.
Chevrons	-	Continuous Vs forming a zig-zag pattern. In fashion c1130 - 1200.
Clerestory	-	An upper level or storey pierced by windows to light the floor below.
Crossing Tower	-	A tower built upon four arches in the middle of a cruciform church.
Cruciform Church	-	A cross-shaped church with transeptal chapels forming the arms of the cross.
Cusp	-	A projecting point between the foils of a foiled Gothic arch.
Dado	-	A decorative (usually blank arcaded) lower part of a wall or screen.
Decorated	-	The architectural style in vogue in England c1300 - 1380
Easter Sepulchre	-	A recess in a chancel north wall which received an effigy of Christ at Easter.
Elizabethan	-	Of the time of Queen Elizabeth I (1558 - 1603).
Fan Vault	-	Vault with fan-like patterns. In fashion from c1440 to 1530.
Foil	-	A lobe formed by the cusping of a circle or an arch.
Four-centred Arch	-	A low flattish arch with each of two curves drawn from two compass points.
Hammerbeam Roof	-	Roof carried on arched braces set on beams projecting from a wall.
Head-stops	-	Heads of humans, animals or mythical beasts forming ends of a hoodmould.
Hoodmould	-	A projecting moulding above a lintel or arch to throw off water.
Impost	-	A wall bracket, often moulded, to support an arch.
Jacobean	-	Of the time of when King James I (1603 - 25.)
Jamb	-	The side of a doorway, window or other opening.
King Post	-	An upright timber beam connecting a collar-beam with a tie-beam.
Lancet	-	A long and comparatively narrow window usually with a pointed head.
Light	-	A compartment of a window.
Lintel	-	A horizontal stone or beam spanning an opening.
Low-side window	-	A window with a low sill allowing anyone outside a chancel to see the altar.
Miserichord	-	A bracket underneath a hinged choir stall seat to support a standing person.
Mullion	-	A vertical member dividing the lights of a window.
Nave	-	The part of a church in which the congregation sits (or stood originally).
Norman	-	A division of English Romanesque architecture from 1066 to c1200.
Ogival Arch	-	Arch of oriental origin with both convex and concave curves.
Pediment	-	Low pitched gable over an end wall or a doorway or a window.
Perpendicular	-	The architectural style in vogue in England c1370 - 1540.
Pilaster	-	Flat buttress or pier attached to a wall.
Piscina	-	A stone basin used for washing out holy vessels after a mass.
Plinth	-	The projecting base of a wall.
Quoin	-	A dressed stone at the corner of a building.
Rere-arch	-	An inner arch such as the internal arch over a window or doorway opening.
Respond	-	A half pier or column bonded into a wall and carrying one end of an arch.
Reticulation	-	Tracery with a net-like appearance. In fashion c1330 - 70.
Rood Screen	-	A screen with a crucifix mounted upon it between a nave and a chancel.
Sedilia	-	Seats for clergy (usually three) in the south wall of a chancel or chapel.
Sheela-na-gig	-	A female fertility symbol with the legs wide open to display the vulva.
Spandrel	-	The surface between two arches, or between an arch and a frame or wall.
Squint	-	Opening allowing the main altar to be seen from a subsidiary altar.
Tie-beam	-	A beam connecting the slopes of a roof at or near its foot.
Tracery	-	Intersecting ribwork forming patterns inn the upper part of a Gothic window.
Transom	-	A horizontal member dividing upper and lower lights of a window.
Tuscan	-	An order of Classical architecture.
Tympanum	-	The D-shaped space between the lintel of a doorway and an arch above it.
Venetian Window	-	Window with a square-headed light on either side of an arched main light.
Victorian	-	Of the time of Queen Victoria (1837 - 1901).
Wind-braces	-	Wooden struts used to strengthen the sloping sides of a gabled timber roof.